'Another step into my Kitchen'

by
Evelyn Curtis

First published in 2006 by Evelyn Curtis

ISBN 0-9539806-3-4

Cover photograph
Courtesy of the Suffolk Free Press

Photography by
Evelyn Curtis and Dominic Shaw

Designed and printed by
The Lavenham Press, Lavenham, Suffolk CO10 9RN

DEDICATION

This book is dedicated to my family, and to all 'My Ladies' of the 21st Ladies Luncheon Club, who share my love of good food and good company.

ACKNOWLEDGEMENTS

My sincere thanks in helping me to write this book must go to Cyril, my wonderful husband, and my dear daughter Belinda who always hits on the right note when I am stuck for a word. To my family and friends for all their love and encouragement. To Georgina Ashley at Waitrose, Brackenell for her faith in my book, Paul Reeley, Manager at Sudbury's Waitrose, for his help in getting my book launched in his supermarket; Doreen Brinkley for being my 'other ear' on launch day; Marcia Davis, Suffolk Free Press, for her help with the book cover and Sheila Morley Smith for her help in marketing my books. A special thank you to David Tokeley for his enthusiasm, patience and humour in compiling my book for print, and to the Lavenham Press Team, who have now seen me through my fourth cookbook with the same patience and understanding.

I have credited recipes that were sent to me where possible, but if there are any that should be credited to someone unknown to me, please let me know so that I can rectify this in any future edition. My thanks also go to anyone I may have unintentionally omitted to mention here.

Evelyn Curtis

INTRODUCTION

When I began writing this book I started off by concentrating on low calorie recipes, aimed solely for would be slimmers. But I soon realised that most of us are now educated in eating less fat, while still providing good nourishing food for our families, and I decided it was best to leave slimming and dieting to those more qualified than me to write on the subject.

Having said this, you will find many perennial favourites that you will recognise in this book, and recipes that make for a healthy diet as well as catering for the heartiest of appetites. Today we have so many choices of fruit and vegetables available to us that we do not have to wait for the seasons to produce strawberries in June and asparagus in May, as both can be flown to us from other countries. But as we all know, and I've written this so many times, there is nothing to beat our own home-grown vegetables and fruit, which reminds us just how much is still grown on our small island. So why eat new potatoes and strawberries all year round, when you can wait for the best of the local crop, food that is produced by local farmers, picked fresh from the fields the morning you buy it, and hasn't had to be chemically treated or preserved to survive journeys of thousands of miles to get to us.

I hope that my book will help keep excitement alive in our food and cooking and that it will be seen as a celebration of all that is locally produced and will introduce you and your families to some delicious new recipes.

Evelyn Curtis.

CONTENTS

STARTERS

A first course can, if it's too heavy or cream laden, spoil the rest of a meal, and I think it best to serve a starter that is light and low in calories. Yoghurt can take the place of cream cheese, and low fat curd cheese makes an ideal alternative, especially when flavoured with seasonings and herbs.

Tuna Salad

KIPPER PÂTE

Although I usually serve this as a starter it does make a delicious sandwich filling, and it freezes well too.

Serves 4.

300g (10½ oz) kipper fillets, boned and skinned

110g (4 oz) carton cottage cheese

1 clove garlic, skinned

Juice of ½ lemon

Fresh ground black pepper

¼ teaspoon grated nutmeg

1 tablespoon natural yoghurt

Slices of lemon to garnish

Soak the kipper fillets in a little hot water for a few minutes to remove any excess salt, and then drain. Liquidise all the ingredients, adding the kipper fillets last, you should end up with an appetising smooth pâté. Garnish with lemon twists and a little parsley to add colour to the pâté.

STUFFED TOMATOES

You will need really large firm tomatoes for this recipe, and in the summer I find they travel easily for picnics in the countryside or on the beach.

Serves 6.

6 large tomatoes

225g (8 oz) carton of cottage cheese with chives

1 teaspoon chopped capers (optional)

3 spring onions

1 large hard-boiled egg

110g (4 oz) prawns, chopped

1 teaspoon mild chilli sauce

Good pinch of black pepper

Good pinch of salt

1 tablespoon chopped parsley

Choose really firm tomatoes and slice off the tops, scooping out seeds. Save the pulp to go into soups. Sprinkle the insides with salt and leave to drain upside down for 25 minutes. Mix the cottage cheese with capers, chopped spring onions and egg. Stir in salt and pepper, chilli sauce, prawns and parsley. Spoon the stuffing into the tomatoes and top on the lids. Serve with a crisp green salad.

CHICKEN AND MELON SALAD

Melon in a salad of any kind is refreshing, especially during the summer

months. It's so versatile too, and can be used in a variety of desserts and main courses. When I have any leftover cooked chicken I often make this starter, but serve it as a light lunch.

Serves 4.

1 Honeydew or Galia Melon

450g (1lb) cold cooked chicken

2 green peppers

6 tablespoons low-fat mayonnaise

2 tablespoons chopped mint

Salt, pepper and paprika

Scoop out the flesh of the melon, discard pips and put into a bowl. Cut chicken into small pieces. Slice peppers thinly. Then add the rest of the ingredients to the chicken pieces, season and toss until well mixed. Garnish with mint leaves and sprinkle over paprika.

DATE AND CHICORY STARTER

Crisp chicory makes a refreshing start to a meal, and served in individual dishes it looks both colourful and tempting, especially if you are serving it to guests.

Serves 4.

200g (7 oz) dates, with stones removed

4 ruby grapefruits

2 fairly ripe pears

450g (1lb) chicory

1 lemon

225g (8 oz) natural yoghurt

Salt and pepper

2 tablespoons of port

1 tablespoon honey

Slice the dates, taking out the stones. Remove all the peel and pith from the grapefruits, and take out the segments carefully, saving the juices. Peel, core and slice the pears and combine with the dates, grapefruit and juices in a bowl. Wash and trim the chicory and separate the leaves. Divide between four individual dishes. Grate a little lemon rind for garnish and squeeze the juice and add to the fruit with salt and pepper to taste. Spoon the fruit and juices into dishes over the chicory leaves. Mix together the yoghurt, port and honey and spoon over the salad just before serving. Garnish with the grated lemon rind.

MY VERY LIGHT CHEESE SOUFFLÉ

To make a cheese soufflé the traditional way means using butter and creamy milk as well as full fat Cheddar cheese, so in this recipe I've replaced all the

ingredients with reduced fat ones, which produces a really low fat and calorie reduced soufflé.

Serves 6.

110g (4 oz) reduced fat Cheddar cheese, grated
4 size 2 eggs, separated
1 extra egg white, size 2
2 tablespoons Parmesan cheese
200ml (7 fl oz) skimmed milk
1 small onion, peeled and sliced
1 small carrot, peeled and chopped
25g (1 oz) low fat spread

1 teaspoon oil for greasing
1 bay leaf
4 peppercorns
2 tablespoons plain flour
2 teaspoons Dijon mustard
Pinch of cayenne pepper
Salt and ground black pepper

Grease a 1½ litre (2 pint) soufflé dish and sprinkle with half the Parmesan cheese. Add the carrots, onions, bay leaf and peppercorns to the milk and bring slowly to the boil. Strain and reserve and set aside the milk. Melt the low fat spread in saucepan over a low heat and stir in the flour, mustard and seasoning. Then gradually add the infused milk into the flour mixture, stirring and gradually bringing to the boil. Cool and then beat in 4 egg yolks, using a whisk. Stir in three quarters of the grated cheese and the remaining Parmesan. Whisk egg whites until soft peaks, and using a metal spoon fold in 2 tablespoons of the whites into the sauce. Then gently pour the sauce over the remaining egg whites, gently folding egg whites and sauce together. Pour mixture into soufflé dish, sprinkle with reserved cheese, and bake in preheated oven 180C, 350F, Gas Mark 4 for 35-45 minutes until golden brown, well risen and firm to touch. Serve immediately.

SMOKED MACKEREL PÂTÉ

This pâté can be whipped up in next to no time, and needs very little effort to assemble.

Serves 4.

225g (8 oz) smoked mackerel fillets
3 tablespoons lemon juice
110g (4 oz) low fat spread (Flora or Anchor)

2 tablespoons low fat fromage frais
Freshly ground black pepper to taste

Skin and mince the mackerel. Put all the ingredients into a liquidiser or beat well. Put in a bowl or individual dishes and chill. Garnish with a slice of lemon and serve with thin toast.

STUFFED GREEN PEPPERS

Peppers make delicious starters, but be sure to choose peppers which can stand upright in your cooking dish. The mixture can also be used to fill large tomatoes – you don't need to peel them, as the skin will stop them bursting.

200g (7 oz) long grain rice

2 tablespoons finely chopped parsley

2 onions finely chopped

35g (1½ oz) currants

35g (1½ oz) pine nuts

2 medium sized tomatoes, skinned and chopped

8 large green peppers

2 tablespoons finely chopped mint

¼ teaspoon freshly ground black pepper

1 teaspoon salt

400ml (14 floz) cold water

75g (3 oz) breadcrumbs

150ml (¼ pint) olive oil

Serves 4.

Rinse rice well in a sieve and tip into a bowl, cover with cold water and soak for 1 hour, then drain in sieve. Put 100ml (4 fl oz) oil in a frying pan and add the onions, cook over medium heat until transparent. Add the rice and cook for 1-2 minutes, stirring continuously. Then add the currants, pine nuts, salt, pepper, mint and parsley. Stir well then add the tomatoes and water. Bring to the boil, stirring, then turn the heat down to a slow simmer and cook until the rice is half tender (about 10 minutes). Cut around stalks and remove core on peppers and set aside. Fill the pepper hollows with rice mixture, cover with tops and place in an oiled dish. Well drizzle each pepper with oil and sprinkle over the breadcrumbs. Bake in preheated oven 180C, 350F, Gas Mark 4 for about 45 minutes.   If kept in a refrigerator these stuffed peppers will keep well and can be heated up the next day.

TUNA BEAN SALAD WITH YOGHURT DRESSING

This starter is very low caloried, and if you don't like tuna, tinned salmon works just as well in this recipe.

Serves 4.

110g (4 oz) green beans, sliced

4 medium tomatoes, quartered

200g (7 oz) can tuna in brine

150ml (5fl oz) natural yoghurt

Cook the green beans in boiling salted water for about 4-5 minutes, drain and rinse in cold water. Drain and flake the tuna, then toss with beans and the quartered tomatoes and divide between four plates. Chop and stir a tablespoon of capers into the yoghurt. Add pepper and salt and drizzle over the bean salad.

CRACKED WHEAT AND TOMATO SALAD

A friend gave me this recipe, and in the summer months I often keep a bowl of it in my fridge. It keeps well for at least 5 days and if you double up on the quantities of ingredients it will make a substantial starter for a dinner or buffet party.

Serves 4.

110g (4 oz) cracked wheat	50g (2 oz) peeled and chopped onion
3 large tomatoes, chopped	50ml (2 fl oz) olive oil
75g (3 oz) chopped spring onions	¼ teaspoon low-sodium salt
175g (6 oz) chopped parsley	½ teaspoon black pepper
1 tablespoon chopped mint	200ml (7 fl oz) lemon juice

Put cracked wheat into a large bowl and pour enough hot water to cover it, and let it stand for 25-30 minutes. Drain the wheat in a sieve or colander. Combine the wheat, tomatoes, spring onions and the rest of the ingredients in a large bowl, mixing well. Add the oil, salt, pepper and lemon juice. Stir the mixture well, then cover and refrigerate until required.

STUFFED PEARS

A refreshing light starter, and if you want to make it less calorific, leave out the chopped walnuts and just put one almond flake in the centre of each pear for decoration.

Serves 4.

2 ripe pears, halved	25g (1 oz) chopped walnuts
110g (4 oz) cottage cheese	¼ sliced, unpeeled cucumber
50g (2 oz) seeded green grapes	Lettuce leaves

Sprinkle a little lemon juice over pear halves. Scoop out flesh, removing core. Mix cheese with pear flesh and walnuts. Add grapes. Stuff pear halves with mixture and sprinkle a little paprika over the tops. Place half a pear on each serving plate and garnish with a ring of cucumber slices and lettuce leaves. Scoop out the flesh of the melon, discard pips and put into a bowl. Cut chicken into small pieces. Slice peppers thinly. Then add the rest of the ingredients to the chicken pieces, season and toss until well mixed. Garnish with mint leaves and sprinkle over paprika.

SOUPS

Soup is one of the most nourishing meals you can have. It can be made well in advance and stored covered in a refrigerator for at least 4 days. It's always a good idea to make double quantities of soup so that you can store a supply in the freezer, but remember to thaw slowly and reheat gently. Using a little low fat spread or oil to sweat the vegetables is much better than using butter, and is less fattening, or you can leave out fat altogether and just use a good stock base for the soup.

The soups in this chapter are varied and colourful, and most economical to serve. Some are robust enough to serve as a main course with crusty bread or toasted croutons, and soup makes a satisfying first course or lunch, and is ideal for a light supper meal.

Potato and Leek Soup

TOMATO AND PEPPER SOUP

When tomatoes are in season and they are in plentiful supply this is a good way of using them up.

Serves 4.

450g (1lb) tomatoes, skinned and sliced
2 red peppers, sliced
1 medium onion, peeled and sliced
1 tablespoon plain flour

1 tablespoon oil
850ml (1½ pints) chicken stock (or cube)
Salt and pepper
1 tablespoon chopped parsley

Heat the oil in a thick saucepan. Add the sliced vegetables and sauté for 6 minutes. Stir in the flour and gradually add the stock. Bring to the boil and simmer for 20 minutes. Liquidise or rub through a sieve. Season to taste and sprinkle over the chopped parsley.

CELERY SOUP

This soup can be made in three easy steps. Try to use a good chicken stock for flavour if you can.

Serves 4-6.

225g (8 oz) carrots, scraped and chopped
6 sticks of celery
1 large potato, peeled and chopped
1 large onion, peeled and chopped

600ml (1 pint) semi-skimmed milk
850ml (1½ pints) chicken stock
Salt and pepper
1½ tablespoons chopped parsley

Place all chopped vegetables into a large saucepan with stock, milk and seasoning. Bring to the boil and simmer for 25-30 minutes. Remove from heat and sieve or liquidise. Sprinkle over chopped parsley for garnish.

FRESH PEA SOUP

This soup definitely benefits by using fresh peas instead of frozen or tinned, and you can almost taste the newness of the peas with each mouthful!

Serves 6.

450g (1lb) fresh peas, shelled

1 large onion, peeled and chopped

1 medium lettuce, roughly torn

1 litre (1¾ pints) vegetable stock

150ml (5 fl oz) yoghurt

Put all the ingredients into a heavy saucepan and simmer in the liquid for 25-30 minutes, until the shelled peas are cooked. Liquidise until smooth. Add the yoghurt to a little of the soup, then combine this mixture with the rest of the soup. Reheat without boiling or the yoghurt may curdle. Should yield about 1½ litres (2 pints).

MIXED VEGETABLE SOUP

This is a filling vegetable soup, and you will probably have most of the ingredients in your store cupboard, and if you want to make a substantial main meal, you can always add a few ounces of cooked pasta or a toasted croutons.

Serves 4-6.

1 carrot, peeled and finely chopped

2 sticks of celery, chopped

2 medium onions, peeled and chopped

2 small potatoes, peeled and chopped

3 tomatoes, skinned and chopped

2 small leeks, washed and chopped

Half a green cabbage, finely chopped

1 small turnip, peeled and chopped

2 garlic cloves, peeled and crushed

850ml (1½ pints) good meat stock

(or beef cube)

1 tablespoon olive oil

Salt and pepper

Heat oil in a large heavy saucepan and lightly fry the carrot, celery, onion, turnip, potato and garlic until they are soft. Heat the stock in a separate saucepan and then add to the vegetables, cover and simmer for about 10-15 minutes or until the vegetables are cooked. Add the tomatoes, leeks and cabbage and bring back to the boil. Simmer for a further 15 minutes, season to taste and serve.

BROAD BEAN AND MINT SOUP

Nothing is better than herbs picked fresh from the garden, but if you make this soup in winter time then dried mint will work just as well, and if want to make the soup more colourful, sprinkle a little paprika over the top of each serving.

Serves 4-6.

750g (1lb 10 oz) broad beans, shelled

1 tablespoon olive oil

2 small onions, peeled and chopped

1 litre (1¾ pints) vegetable stock

2 tablespoons fresh mint, chopped

5 tablespoons fromage frais

Grated rind and juice of ½ lemon

1 garlic clove, peeled and chopped

Salt and pepper to taste

Fresh mint leaves to garnish

Heat the oil in a large saucepan and fry the onion and garlic for about 5 minutes until softened. Add the beans to the pan and fry for 2 minutes. Add all the remaining ingredients, except the fromage frais, and bring to a steady boil. Cover and simmer for 15-20 minutes until the beans are cooked. Purée the soup in a liquidiser or food processor, or you can pass through a sieve. Return to the saucepan, add the fromage frais and heat for only 5 minutes, taking care not to bring to the boil. Serve garnished with mint sprigs. This soup can also be served chilled, and is delicious in summertime.

PUMPKIN AND CURRY SOUP

A warming winter soup, just right for serving on Hallowe'en or Bon-fire night, when you can double up the quantity of ingredients for extra servings.

Serves 6.

700g (1½ 1lb) pumpkin flesh

350g (12 oz) celeriac, peeled and chopped

1.8 litres (3 pints) vegetable stock

1½ teaspoons milk curry paste

25g (1 oz) butter

Salt and pepper to taste

Place the prepared vegetables and stock in a large heavy saucepan, gradually stir in the curry paste and bring to the boil. Simmer for 25 minutes until the vegetables are cooked. Put into a blender or food processor and blend until smooth. Return to pan and gradually heat until it's reached almost boiling point. Stir or whisk in butter until thoroughly blended into the soup. Serve immediately piping hot.

HEARTY BEAN SOUP

A hearty satisfying soup for a hungry family, doesn't take long to prepare and cook and is low in calories too.

Serves 4.

1 clove garlic, crushed

1 bunch spring onions, sliced

150g (5 oz) whole-wheat pasta shells

450g (1lb) can Soya or butter beans

1 tablespoon oil

175g (6 oz) carrots

1 litre (1¾ pints) vegetable stock

1 tablespoon vegetable purée

3 tablespoons chopped parsley

110g (4 oz) celery, cleaned and chopped

Salt and pepper

Heat the oil in a large saucepan. Lightly fry the crushed garlic and spring onions for 3-5 minutes until soft. Peel and chop the carrots, add to the saucepan with stock and vegetable purée. Bring to the boil and add the pasta shells, drained can of Soya or butter beans, chopped parsley and chopped celery. Bring back to the boil, cover and simmer for about 15-20 minutes until the vegetables are cooked. Season to taste and serve hot.

TURNIP AND ONION SOUP

This is a smooth soup, using just turnips and onions together, and without the addition of meat, which would turn it into a stew, gives a nutty root flavour.

Serves 4-6.

1¼ kg (2¾ lb) white turnips, peeled and diced

3 large onions, peeled and chopped

2 garlic cloves, peeled and chopped

1 litre (1¾ pints) chicken stock

1 bay leaf

5fl oz (¼ pint) skimmed milk

Salt and white pepper

Put turnips, onion and garlic into a large saucepan and slowly bring to the boil. Skim the top. Simmer covered on a low heat until the turnips and onions are tender. When cool, purée the soup in a liquidizer and return to the saucepan. Stir in the milk and season to taste. Reheat gradually and serve piping hot. This soup will keep well in the refrigerator.

SPLIT PEA SOUP

This recipe uses quite a lot of ingredients, but it's well worth assembling them all to make this nourishing, yet surprisingly, low fat soup. You will see I've topped each serving with a little low-fat sour cream, but the soup looks just as appetising without it.

Serves 6.

350g (12 oz) green split peas

2 teaspoons olive oil

225g (8 oz) onion, peeled and chopped

½ teaspoon black pepper

1 tablespoon tomato paste

1 tablespoon soy sauce

175g (6 oz) carrot, scraped and chopped

3 garlic cloves, peeled and chopped

1 bay leaf

1 tablespoon finely chopped rosemary

1 teaspoon paprika

1½ litres (2 pints) water

425ml (¾ pint) vegetable stock

200ml (7fl oz) low-fat sour cream

50g (2 oz) chopped parsley

1 teaspoon salt

Wash peas, cover with water and set aside. Heat 1 teaspoon oil in large saucepan. Add onion, carrot and bay leaf, and fry gently for about 5 minutes, stirring. Add 2 teaspoons garlic, 1 teaspoon rosemary, paprika and pepper and cook for 5 minutes. Add tomato paste and soy sauce, cook until liquid reduces to brown bits and scrape the pan to loosen bits. Drain peas and add peas to pan. Add water, vegetable stock to onion mixture and gradually bring to the boil. Cover and reduce heat to medium-low. Simmer for 1 hour, stirring often. Take out bay leaf. Place half the soup in a blender or food processor and blend until smooth. Pour puréed soup into a bowl and repeat this process with remaining soup. Add 1 teaspoon oil, 1 teaspoon garlic, 2 teaspoon rosemary and parsley. Gently heat again and spoon soup into bowls, topping each serving with a little of the sour cream (optional).

VEGETABLE STOCK

Try making your own vegetable stock, the flavour it produces is well worth the time and effort, and you can always make a good supply in advance and freeze it until required.

Yields about 2 litres (3½ pints)

1 teaspoon olive oil

110g (4 oz) onion, peeled and chopped

175g (6 oz) carrot, scraped and chopped

3 large leeks, cleaned and chopped

110g (4 oz) mushrooms, sliced

50g (2 oz) chopped parsley

½ teaspoon salt

3 sprigs of thyme

2 bay leaves

2 litres (3½ pints) water

Heat oil in a large heavy saucepan over a medium heat. Add onion and carrot and fry gently for about 10 minutes. Add prepared leeks, mushrooms and remaining ingredients to the onion mixture and slowly bring back to the boil. Reduce heat and simmer until liquid is reduced to about 2 litres (3½ pints). This stock makes a nourishing stew with meat added, or it can simply be used on its own as a very low caloried soup.

FISH

I read somewhere that if you coat fish with a thin layer of mayonnaise it will keep it moist when grilling, and as all my fish is cooked in my Aga oven, it works very well for me. I always use low fat mayonnaise or make my own by mixing 3 tablespoons of low fat yoghurt with 1½ tablespoons of mustard, black pepper and a squeeze of lemon juice. This mixture also makes a delicious sauce to serve with most fish dishes too.

Apart from being low in fat and calories, you can do so much with fish, especially now there is such a wide variety in our fishmongers and on super market counters. And if you are lucky enough to be able to get freshly caught fish, then there is nothing to beat it.

Cod Steak with Carrots and Beans

SMOKED MACKEREL WITH COURGETTES AND CELERY

Courgettes are especially good for people watching their calorie intake, and can be used in many dishes, and although this dish uses rice, it is still very low in calories and fat.

Serves 4.

110g (4 oz) courgettes, sliced

2 large smoked mackerel fillets (supermarkets sell these in packets, already boned and skinned)

175g (6 oz) long grain rice

2 small peppers (1 red and 1 green), sliced thinly

1 medium onion, peeled and chopped

4 stalks celery, sliced

425ml (¾ pint) chicken or vegetable stock

Juice of 1 lemon

1 tablespoon olive oil

Salt and freshly ground black pepper

Heat the oil in a large heavy frying pan and lightly fry the onion, celery and peppers, taking care not to let them brown. Add rice and stir, absorbing all the oil. Add stock and salt and pepper and cook for a further 15 minutes. Add courgettes and cook for a further 6 minutes. The rice should now be cooked and all the juices absorbed. Flake the mackerel and stir into rice mixture with the lemon juice. Heat for a further few minutes, pile on to four individual plates, or a serving dish, sprinkle over the chopped parsley. You can serve this dish either hot or cold.

PLAICE AND CRISPY BACON

This is such a simple dish to make, and the combination of bacon with fish makes it less bland. I've used plaice in this recipe, but you can use almost any other white fish.

Serves 4.

4 large plaice fillets

4 rashers of bacon with fat trimmed off

1½ tablespoons olive oil

2 tablespoons chopped dill (fresh or dried)

1 red pepper, seeded & chopped

4-5 tablespoons fresh orange juice

Make sure as much fat and rind as possible is trimmed off the bacon, and chop into small pieces. Fry bacon in non-stick pan until crisp. Mix the oil, juice and three quarters of the dill and red pepper together with the cooked bacon, season to taste and warm through. Clean and dry plaice fillets, make three slashes across each fillet, brush grill pan with a little oil and heat under grill for about half a minute. Arrange fish on the grill pan and brush with a little warm oil and grill for about 6 minutes, adding some of the bacon and pepper mixture halfway through cooking time. Put onto hot serving plates and top with bacon and pepper mixture. Sprinkle with remaining dill or some chopped parsley. New potatoes and sliced courgettes go well with this fish dish.

SALMON RISOTTO

Use red salmon for this recipe – I find the red tinned Alaska salmon I get from my local super market is ideal for this recipe, and if you have any left over it will reheat next day.

Serves 4.

425g (15oz) tinned red salmon
1 litre (1¾ pints) hot vegetable stock
400g (14 oz) chopped tomatoes
1 tablespoon olive oil
1 medium onion, peeled and chopped
1 green pepper, deseeded and chopped
225g (8 oz) packet balsamic wild rice mix

2 cloves garlic, chopped
10g (½ oz) low fat spread
Juice of 1 lemon
2 tablespoons fresh parsley, chopped

Drain salmon, remove skin and bones and flake into a bowl. Set aside. Melt the oil and half fat spread in a non-stick pan, add the onion, garlic and pepper. Fry gently for a few minutes until softened. Remove from the pan and set aside. Add rice to the pan and cook for a further 3 minutes. Gradually stir in all of the hot stock and bring to the boil. Add lemon juice and tomatoes and simmer for 15 minutes, continually stirring until nearly all the stock is absorbed. Add the salmon and cooked pepper, garlic and onion, and simmer for a further 5 minutes until the stock has been absorbed. Stir in the parsley, season to taste and serve garnished with lemon slices and chopped parsley.

MIXED SEAFOOD SALAD

For this recipe you can either make up your own mixed seafood selection, or buy a selection from your local super market. Serve in one of your daintiest glass bowls with plenty of green salad.

Serves 4.

225g (8 oz) mixed seafood selection
110g (4 oz) cockles, cleaned and shelled

1 green pepper, deseeded & chopped
1 yellow pepper, deseeded & chopped

110g (4oz) winkles, shelled

275g (9½ oz) king prawns

12 cherry tomatoes

Lettuce leaves to line bowl

1 red pepper, deseeded and chopped

Dressing:

2 tablespoons olive oil

½ teaspoon honey

½ teaspoon Dijon mustard

Freshly ground black pepper

2 tablespoons white wine vinegar

Freshly chopped parsley

Place the seafood selection in a bowl with the cockles and winkles. Halve the cherry tomatoes and add the chopped peppers and king prawns. Mix the dressing ingredients together with a whisk. Then line a glass serving bowl with lettuce and spoon in the seafood. Pour over the dressing and serve immediately.

HADDOCK FILLETS WITH DILL AND THYME

An easy dish to prepare. Try to use fresh fillets if you can, but if you do buy frozen make sure they are thoroughly defrosted before using. Almost any fresh herbs can be used, but I think dill and thyme together give the dish a really piquant flavour.

Serves 4.

450g (1lb) fish fillets, haddock or cod

1 teaspoon chopped dill & thyme use fresh

1 tablespoon lemon juice

herbs if possible

1½ teaspoons unsaturated margarine, melted

Freshly ground black pepper

Arrange the fillets in baking dish. Mix the lemon juice, margarine and herbs together and spoon over fish. Sprinkle lightly with pepper. Bake in preheated oven 230C, 450F, Gas Mark 8 for 10 minutes. Sprinkle with fresh herbs and serve with jacket potato.

HERBY PLAICE FILLETS

This is a very easy dish to make and it can be ready, cooked and on the table in no time at all, especially if you make your own breadcrumbs and chop the parsley in a blender.

Serve 4.

4 medium plaice fillets

5g (1 oz) breadcrumbs

1 tablespoon low fat margarine, melted

10g (½ oz) chopped fresh parsley

1 teaspoon fresh or dried thyme

½ teaspoon ground black pepper

In a shallow dish place the fillets in a single layer. Mix the breadcrumbs, margarine, parsley, thyme and pepper together, and then sprinkle over the fish. Bake uncovered in preheated oven 230C, 450F, Gas Mark 8 for about 20 - 25 minutes.

SALMON STEAKS WITH YOGHURT AND WATERCRESS SAUCE

If you want a light summer meal then fresh salmon is ideal. In this recipe you can either bake or poach the salmon steaks, or cook in the microwave, but if you cook by the latter remember not to overcook otherwise the fish will be dry and tasteless.

Serves 4.

4 fairly thick salmon steaks

1 tablespoon lemon juice

Watercress to garnish

2 tablespoons fresh chopped parsley

1 tablespoon chopped spring onions

For the sauce:

300g (10½ oz) low fat cottage cheese

25g (1 oz) chopped watercress leaves

50g (2 oz) low fat natural yoghurt

Lightly oil a large piece of foil and arrange the steaks in a single layer. Sprinkle over the lemon juice, add seasoning to taste. Fold over the foil and place on a baking tray and bake in preheated oven 200C, 400F, Gas Mark 6 for about 20 minutes, making sure the fish is cooked. Combine all the sauce ingredients together in a blender and process until well mixed. Arrange salmon on individual plates, garnish with sprigs of watercress and serve sauce separately.

SALMON AND CRAB FISH CAKES

If you've any left over fish then fishcakes are a good way of using it up. But in this recipe I have used tinned salmon and crab, but of course you can always use fresh salmon if you want to serve them for a special meal or occasion.

Serves 4-6.

400g (14 oz) tin of red salmon

110g (4 oz) tin of crab meat

300g (10½ oz) mashed potatoes

110g (4 oz) butter

4 teaspoons parsley, chopped

2 small eggs lightly beaten

Breadcrumbs

A little oil for frying

Salt and freshly ground black pepper

Place the fish, potato, butter and parsley into a large bowl. Combine together and season to taste. Form into 6-8 fishcakes, dip into the beaten egg and then into the breadcrumbs. Pour two generous tablespoons of olive oil into a large frying pan, and when it is smoky hot add the fish cakes, lower the heat and cook for at least 5 minutes on each side until firm, crisp and golden. Serve with a green salad and tartare sauce and lemon wedges.

FILLETS OF MACKEREL WITH MUSTARD & HERB SAUCE

The mustard and herb sauce blends well with the oiliness of the mackerel, and you can cook the mackerel early in the day, make the sauce later, ready to serve for an evening meal.

Serves 4.

4 large mackerel fillets,

or whole medium mackerel

Freshly ground pepper

Olive oil

For the sauce:

Salt

75g (3oz) butter

1½ teaspoons white wine or tarragon vinegar

2 tablespoons Dijon mustard

2 egg yolks

2 tablespoons chopped fresh herbs

Blend mustard with the egg yolks and the vinegar, add salt and pepper to taste. Soften the butter until almost melted, making sure it doesn't get too oily. Mix it very gradually into the mustard, egg and vinegar mixture until it has the consistency of mayonnaise. Stir in the chopped herbs. If you cooked the mackerel whole then scrape the skin off the backbone of each fish. Serve the fish cold with the mustard sauce, and a crisp green salad.

TROUT WITH HORSERADISH AND GARLIC

If you prefer mackerel, which is cheaper, it works just as well, and although I've given double cream as an alternative to the fromage frais, it's still a very low fat dish and high in protein.

Serves 4.

4 smoked trout
4 slices white bread
4 cloves garlic, peeled
50g (2 oz) fresh horseradish or
2 tablespoons bottled

150ml (¼ pint) fromage frais or
double cream
Curly endive lettuce

Remove crusts from bread and dice. Heat oil in frying pan, add garlic cloves and fry bread until golden. Remove and drain well. Discard garlic. Grate horseradish finely, or use the bottled horseradish. Mix the horseradish with the fromage frais or the whipped cream. Wash and trim the endive, use about half and pull into sprigs. Toss the endive with the croutons and arrange on serving plates. Fillet fish, if not already filleted and serve with the salad and horseradish sauce.

CRAB AND TUNA FISHCAKES WITH A TWIST OF BLACK CRACKED PEPPER

This recipe came to me by way of Stephen Thurlow. Stephen runs The Fishcake Company and supplies London stores like Fortnum & Mason and Harvey Nichols as well as main outlets in Suffolk. Once you've tasted a mouthful at one of the many local tastings, you are hooked, and I very often buy a batch to cook or store in my freezer. But try this recipe if you want to have a go at making your own, they are not only delicious, but will keep for five months in the freezer, and you can cook from frozen.

Makes 4 fishcakes.

150g (5 oz) crab (white meat)
150g (5 oz) cooked tuna, or tinned tuna in brine
110g (4 oz) mashed potato

15ml (1 tablespoon tomato puree)
1 chopped spring onion
50g (2 oz) chopped coriander leaves

Half a lemon, rind and juice
(use other half for garnish)
Breadcrumbs and beaten egg for coating
2 eggs

Salt and pepper to taste
1 teaspoon cracked pepper
50g (2 oz) white breadcrumbs

First crack the pepper using a mill, or pestle and mortar for speed. If you don't have a pestle and mortar place peppercorns in a small plastic bag and use a rolling pin for cracking them. The plastic bag stops the pepper flying around the kitchen! In a large bowl separate the crab and tuna with a fork, and add in the lemon rind, the juice, pepper, chopped spring onion, tomato puree, eggs, breadcrumbs, mashed potato and chopped coriander leaves. Mix well until all the ingredients are combined. Season to taste. Form into four fishcakes, using a ladle or hands (add breadcrumbs and mix again if the mixture is too wet to work). Coat each one with the beaten egg and breadcrumbs. Heat oil or butter in a frying pan, brown both sides of the fish cakes, or bake in preheated oven 180C, 350F. Gas Mark 4 for 20-25 minutes until piping hot throughout. Add 5 minutes if cooking from frozen. Serve with a wedge of lemon or lime and a mixed leaf salad for a light lunch or starter.

MEAT

Although I cook mainly by Aga and it's more successful to roast joints and poultry without fat in an Aga, using lemon juices or a little wine or olive oil, I find it's just as successful cooking this way in an electric or gas cooker. I always make sure I trim off any fat before cooking a joint, and also drain off any fat that has accumulated during the cooking time. There will be plenty of juices still left in the cooking pan to make a rich gravy. If you like your gravy thick then use no more than 1-2 teaspoons of cornflour for thickening. Marinating meat and poultry will tenderise it and it will need less cooking time.

When cooking or browning meat I have used butter and olive oil in many of the recipes in this chapter, but I have used it sparingly, and I find a non-stick frying pan is invaluable to cut down on the fat content when cooking, which proves you can still have a low fat calorie meal without cutting out butter and oil completely.

Beef Casserole

MEAT LOAF WITH AUBERGINES

This meat loaf is a bit different in that the main ingredient is aubergines, but if you want to make it into a vegetarian dish, you can leave out the minced beef and sausage meat and substitute them with mushrooms and vegetables of your choice.

Serves 4-6.

2 large aubergines
225g (8 oz) sausage meat
450g (1lb) lean minced beef or pork
1 tablespoon Worcestershire sauce
1 teaspoon mixed herbs

1 egg, beaten
1 large onion, peeled and finely chopped
2 tablespoons fresh white bread crumbs
Salt and pepper

Prick the skins of the aubergines with a fork and put into a preheated oven 190C, 375F, Gas Mark 5 for 45 minutes until soft. Cool, rinsing under cold water, and peel off the skins. Purée the flesh in a processor. Blend aubergine flesh with the remaining ingredients, and spoon into a greased lkg (2 lb) loaf tin and bake in preheated oven 180C, 350F, Gas Mark 4 for 1¾ hours to 2 hours. Allow to cool and serve with a crisp salad. Makes an excellent sandwich filling.

BEEF MINCE AND TOMATO BAKE

This is a homely comfort food dish, with the tomatoes and herbs giving it a colourful and attractive topping. But if you want to give this dish a more crunchy topping, replace the basil mixture with breadcrumbs mixed with grated cheese and chopped parsley over the sliced tomatoes..

Serves 4.

15g (½ oz) butter
1 garlic clove
2 medium onions, peeled and chopped
450g (1lb) minced beef
200g (7 oz) can chopped tomatoes with herbs
2 tablespoons dry red wine

Salt and pepper
175g (6 oz) cooked rice
4 large tomatoes, sliced
5 tablespoons chopped basil leaves
6 spring onions, chopped

Melt butter in large frying pan and cook onion with crushed garlic until soft, but not browned. Crumble beef into pan and cook for about 10 minutes on a fairly low heat, drain off excess liquid and add chopped tomatoes and wine and cook for a further 15 minutes. Season and stir in the cooked rice. Transfer meat mixture into a baking dish, arrange sliced tomatoes on top with the chopped basil and chopped spring onions. Bake in preheated oven 150C, 300F, Gas Mark 2 for about 20-25 minutes until nicely browned.

SPICY MEATBALLS IN MUSTARD SAUCE

The rich mustardy sauce gives this dish a delicious flavour, and makes a satisfying and very low calorie meal to serve for lunch or supper.

Serves 4.

1 large onion, peeled and chopped	Salt and pepper
450g (1lb) lean minced beef	Flour to coat
4 tablespoons fresh breadcrumbs	1 tablespoon dark soy sauce
1 tablespoon tomato puree	Parsley to garnish
1 teaspoon paprika	1 teaspoon dried thyme

Sauce:

15g (½ oz) butter	15g (½ oz) plain flour
1 teaspoon French mustard	300ml (½ pint) milk

Mix the chopped onion with the beef, breadcrumbs, tomato puree, paprika, thyme and seasoning. Form into small balls, dust with flour, brush over with a soy sauce mixed with a little water and fry in a little heated oil in a large non stick pan. Transfer the meatballs to a serving dish and keep warm. For the sauce, put the butter in 600ml (1pint) jug and cook in microwave oven on High for 30 seconds, stir in flour and the mustard and cook together on High for a further 30 seconds. Remove and stir again.

Then gradually whisk the milk into the flour mixture. Season and cook on High for 3 minutes, whisk thoroughly. Spoon sauce over meat balls and sprinkle over the parsley. Serve with chopped spinach.

HERBY SPARE RIBS

The fruity herb-flavoured sauce makes an unusual change from the usual sweet and sour sauces often used for this dish. Choose meaty spare ribs, and to make easy cooking, ask your butcher to chop them into individual ones for you.

Serves 4.

1kg (2 lb) spare ribs	200ml (7fl oz) dry cider
3 small onions, peeled and chopped	Salt and pepper
2 tablespoons olive oil	3 tablespoons fresh thyme, chopped
2 garlic cloves	3 medium carrots, scraped and chopped
75g (3 oz) sultanas	

Heat oil in a flameproof casserole and fry the ribs, turning often until golden brown. Add onions and fry until lightly browned. Crush garlic and add to the casserole with the carrots, sultanas, cider, seasoning and thyme. Cover and take off heat and transfer to preheated oven 180C, 350F, Gas Mark 4 and cook for 45 minutes. Skim off surplus fat and serve with jacket potatoes and green vegetables of your choice.

BRAISED LIVER AND MUSHROOMS IN SHERRY SAUCE

I think liver and mushrooms are a perfect combination, and the sherry sauce gives the dish a piquant taste, and this dish will freeze well up to 2 months.

Serves 4.

450g (1lb) lambs liver	25g (1 oz) butter
350g (12 oz) button mushrooms	2 teaspoons cornflour
3 small onions, peeled and chopped finely	300ml (½ pint) beef stock cube
1 clove garlic, crushed	4 tablespoons sherry
4 spring onions, chopped	Salt and pepper

Wipe the mushrooms and slice thickly. Melt butter in heavy frying pan and quickly fry and seal the liver on a high heat. Remove and set aside to keep warm. Reduce the heat and add onions, garlic and mushrooms to the pan juices. Cook on a low heat, stirring frequently for 2 minutes, add spring onions and cook for a further 1 minute. Blend the cornflour to a paste with the sherry and pour over the vegetables with the stock. Season to taste. Bring to the boil, stirring, then return the liver to the pan with any juices and heat through for about 4 minutes. Serve with rice.

POT ROAST BEEF WITH ONIONS AND PEPPERS

For Sunday lunch there's nothing to beat British beef, it's so nourishing and full of flavour, and there are so many different dishes and meals you can make to suit almost every occasion. Pot roasts are my favourite, once prepared, you can just pop it into the oven and forget about it until you are ready to serve it, and it makes an appetising Sunday lunch.

Serves 4-6.

1½ kg (3lb 5oz) rolled brisket of beef	3 tablespoons olive oil
½ teaspoon ground allspice	1 teaspoon dried marjoram
2 red and 2 yellow peppers	300ml (½ pint) dry cider
2 medium onions	600ml (1 pint) beef stock cube
2 cloves garlic	15g (½ oz) cornflour
Salt and pepper	

Mix allspice and seasoning together and rub over joint. Crush garlic and slice peppers and onions. Heat oil in a large flameproof casserole dish and brown the joint of beef all over in the hot oil. Add half the peppers and all the onion, garlic and dried marjoram. Cook for 8 minutes until onion is soft. Pour on the cider and stock. Reduce heat, cover and simmer on hot plate for 2-2½ hours until the beef is tender when pierced. Remove beef from casserole and set aside to keep warm. Strain the liquid into a pan, add remaining peppers and cornflour dissolved in 2 tablespoons water and bring to the boil, stirring frequently for 10 minutes until liquid is reduced slightly and lightly thickened. Serve gravy separately with the beef.

PORK CHOPS WITH LEMON AND BAY LEAVES

Bay leaves give a wonderful flavour to this dish – try to use fresh leaves if you can, but dried will work just as well. It's a good idea to start marinating the chops early in the morning of the day you are going to serve them

Serves 4.

4 loin pork chops, fairly thick	1 cup homemade or canned chicken soup
4 tablespoons olive oil	Peeled zest of 1 lemon
4 fresh bay leaves	Salt and freshly ground black pepper

Combine the lemon peel, 3 tablespoons olive oil and the bay leaves together in a shallow dish. Add the pork chops and coat well with the marinade and put one bay leaf under each chop. Cover with cling foil and leave in fridge to marinade for 10-16 hours, turning the chops two or three times. Preheat oven to 190C, 375F, Gas Mark 5. Season pork chops well, and in a large oven-proof dish heat the 4th tablespoon of olive oil and quickly sauté the pork chops over a fairly high heat until they are well browned on each side. Transfer the pan to preheated oven and bake for a further 8-10 minutes. Transfer chops to a serving plate, pouring off the fat in pan, and over a medium heat add stock and remaining lemon peel, thicken with a little cornflour and pour over each chop when serving. Don't eat the bay leaves!

LAMB TENDERLOINS WITH ROSEMARY AND GARLIC

Lamb tenderloins are one of the leanest cuts of meat, and this dish can be prepared early in the day and cooked later, and the whole dish is very low in calories.

Serves 4.

450g (1lb) lamb tenderloins	110g (4 oz) button mushrooms
1½ teaspoons dried peppercorns, crushed	2 tablespoons dry sherry
1 tablespoons fresh rosemary	1 tablespoon light soy sauce
2 cloves garlic, crushed	

Place lamb in a shallow dish. In a small bowl mix peppercorns, rosemary, garlic, sherry and soy sauce, add the wiped sliced mushrooms and pour over the lamb. Cover with cling film and leave to marinate in refrigerator for 1-5 hours. Remove lamb from marinade and grill under hot grill until meat is cooked through. Strain marinade and add any juices from cooked lamb, heat and pour over sliced tenderloins. Serve with broccoli and mashed potatoes.

CORN BEEF HASH

This dish comes from a friend of mine in America and has become a great family favourite. It really doesn't need any accompaniment, although I sometimes serve it with poached eggs arranged on top (one egg for each person).

Serves 6.

225g (8 oz) tinned corn beef, flaked	1 tablespoon tomato puree
350g (12 oz) thinly sliced onions	Salt and pepper to taste

1 tablespoon olive oil

25g (1 oz) butter

450g (1lb) mashed potatoes

Poached eggs (optional)

450g (1lb) finely sliced steamed cabbage

Heat oil and lightly fry sliced onions. Mix onions and all the other ingredients together in a large bowl. Add tomato purée and seasoning. Turn mixture into a meat baking tin, pat into an oval loaf shape and refrigerate until needed. Bake in preheated oven 190C, 375F, Gas Mark 5 for about 30 minutes. Transfer to a serving plate, with the poached eggs arranged on top if you are going to serve them.

LEAN SHEPHERD'S PIE

Shepherd's Pie was always made from leftovers from the Sunday joint, but the traditional Sunday Roast has now been replaced by stir-frys, vegetarian dishes and a host of varied dishes and recipes that have now come into our kitchens. But I usually make my shepherd's pie using the leanest mincemeat I can buy, or making my own mince with a lean cut of beef or lamb. Traditionally, of course, lamb is always used for Shepherd's Pie and beef for Cottage Pie!

Serves 4-6.

450g (1lb) minced beef or lamb

3 small onions, peeled and chopped

2 cloves garlic, crushed

2 small carrots, scraped and minced

3 tablespoons tomato purée

1 teaspoon thyme

450g (1lb) mashed potatoes

Pepper and Salt

1 teaspoon paprika

2 teaspoons Worcestershire sauce

150ml (5 fl oz) water

In a large non-stick frying pan cook the mince beef or lamb, stirring continually until browned, and pour off any surplus fat. Add onions, garlic and carrot and cook until tender. Add tomato purée, water, thyme and Worcestershire sauce. Season to taste and simmer for about 6 minutes. Spoon mixture into a baking dish and spread the mashed potatoes over, sprinkle with paprika and a little grated cheese. Bake in preheated oven 190C, 375F, Gas Mark 5 for 35-40 minutes until thoroughly cooked through. Serve with a green vegetable of your choice.

BEEF AND VEGETABLE CASSEROLE

This casserole is ideal to serve in the winter when there are plenty of root vegetable in shops and on market stalls. The juices from the meat and the

vegetables all combine to make a rich savoury gravy.

Serves 4-6.

1kg (2lb) root vegetables of your choice
3 small onions, peeled
700g (1½ lb) best stewing steak
2 tablespoons plain flour
1 tablespoon olive oil
1½ tablespoons tomato purée

150ml (¼ pint) dry cider
600ml (1 pint) beef cube stock
Grated rind from 1 orange
2 bay leaves
Salt and pepper

Chop one third of the root vegetables and with the onions put into a large ovenproof casserole. Cube the beef and toss in seasoned flour. Heat oil in a large pan and brown the beef, then transfer to the casserole. Season again and add bay leaves, purée and cider. Add the beef stock, cover and simmer in preheated oven 180C, 350F, Gas Mark 4 for 1½ - 2 hours. Chop the remaining vegetables and add to the casserole with finely grated orange rind and a little of the orange juice and cook for a further 25 minutes. Thicken the gravy with a little cornflour and cook for a further 10 minutes. Serve with jacket potatoes and spinach or broccoli.

SAVOURY MEATBALLS

A real hearty dish, full of protein. You can make the meatballs early and leave them in the refrigerator until you are ready to cook them later in the day.

Serves 6.

450g (1lb) lean minced beef
50g (2 oz) porridge oats
1 tablespoon parsley
1 egg, beaten
2 small onions, peeled and finely chopped

2 cloves garlic
2 tablespoons olive oil
400g (14 oz) can of chopped tomatoes
400g (14 oz) can baked beans
400g (14 oz) cannelloni beans

Cover the porridge oats with boiling water and leave to stand for 6-8 minutes until the water is all absorbed. Mix beef, seasoning, finely chopped parsley and the egg. Fry the onions in a little oil and set aside. Squeeze out excess water from the porridge oats and mix into the minced beef. Shape into 16-18 meatballs and fry in the remaining oil. Drain on kitchen paper, and pour out the remaining oil from the pan. Add tomatoes, beans, onions and garlic to the pan, combining thoroughly and adding the meatballs. Heat for about 8 minutes, stirring. Garnish with chopped chives or parsley.

POULTRY AND GAME

Chicken is noted for being very low in fat. Having said that, I always make sure I take off as much of the skin as possible, otherwise a chicken dish can turn out to be a high caloried fat one. I mostly buy jointed chicken, as there are so many different ways it can be cooked, and if there are any left-overs, they can be cut up and used in a salad or sandwiches. In this chapter I've given recipes that use cider, honey and orange, as I find they make excellent marinades. If you baste your chicken joints, or a whole chicken, whilst they are cooking, you will find it gives the meat a delicious flavour, duck is also delicious with honey and orange, as is guinea fowl cooked in cider.

Poussins in Cider

ROAST CHICKEN WITH CUMIN, HONEY AND ORANGE

Combining the honey and orange together with the cumin, gives this chicken dish a delicious flavour, and it's so easy to prepare.

Serves 4.

1 1.4kg (3lb) chicken
1½ tablespoons grated orange rind
¼ teaspoon salt
1 garlic clove, peeled and minced

¼ cup (87g) honey
1 tablespoon ground cumin
A little black pepper

Prepare chicken in usual way, discarding giblets and rinsing chicken with cold water, and trimming excess fat. Starting at neck cavity, loosen skin from breast and drumsticks by inserting fingers, gently pushing between skin and meat. Combine honey and remaining ingredients. Rub honey mixture under loosened skin and over breast and drumsticks, under wing tips and over back. Place chicken, breast side up in large casserole dish or roasting tin. Pierce skin several times with fork or skewer, and bake at 200C, 400F, Gas Mark 6 for 30 minutes, covered loosely with foil. Bake for an additional 40 minutes until crisp and tender. Stand chicken for 10 minutes before carving. Serve with crispy roast potatoes, carrots and a green vegetable.

CHICKEN BAKED WITH SPINACH

The layers of cooked chicken with green vegetables, topped with a creamy cheese sauce make this dish ideal to serve for a family supper or lunch.

Serves 4.

175g (6 oz) cooked chicken
175g (6oz) cooked potatoes
3 leeks
2 sticks celery
2 rashers lean back bacon
15g butter (½ oz) butter

75g (3 oz) spinach leaves
Salt and pepper
3 medium eggs
3 tablespoons Cheddar cheese grated
Milk to mix

Slice the cooked chicken and potatoes, then cover and set aside. Wash and slice the leeks and celery and dice the bacon rashers. Preheat the oven to 190C, 375F, Gas Mark 5. Melt butter in large frying pan and add the leeks, celery and bacon. Cook gently for 2-3 minutes until vegetables begin to soften. Meanwhile, tear the spinach leaves into small pieces. Then layer the chicken, potatoes, spinach and leek mixture in an oven-proof dish, seasoning to taste between the layers. Beat eggs and stir in the cheese with just enough milk to give a pouring consistency. Add a pinch of ground nutmeg and pour over the chicken mixture. Bake for 20-25 minutes until the top is set and golden brown.

POUSSINS IN CIDER

A lovely aromatic casserole that makes a superb dinner for 4 or you can halve all the ingredients and make a special dinner for two!

Serves 4.

4 x 450g (1lb) oven-ready poussins	2 large dessert apples
50g (2 oz) butter	225g (8 oz) cabbage
4 tablespoons wholegrain French mustard	110g (4 oz) spinach leaves
2 teaspoons Worcester sauce	2 tablespoons fresh chopped sage
2 teaspoons lemon juice	600ml (1 pint) dry cider
4 small bulbs fennel	Salt and pepper

Clean and wipe the poussins. Place on their sides, breasts facing, and put into a large casserole. Hold in place with cocktail sticks. Melt butter over low heat, then stir in mustard, Worcester sauce and lemon juice and brush mixture over poussins. Meanwhile, trim and slice the fennel, quarter, core and slice apple, finely shred cabbage and spinach, chop sage. Add fennel, apple and cabbage to casserole. Cover with half the cider and cook for about 40 minutes at 190C, 375F, Gas Mark 5. Then add spinach, seasoning and rest of cider and cook uncovered for a further 10-12 minutes. Serve with jacket potatoes and green beans.

CHICKEN BREASTS IN MUSTARD SAUCE

This dish can be made in advance and heated up when ready to serve, and it's very low in calories.

Serves 4.

450g (1lb) chicken breasts	1 tablespoon mustard
1 orange	200g (7 oz) créme fraîche
Salt and pepper	1 tablespoon cornflour
2 tablespoons vegetable oil	

Peel the orange, remove all pith and cut into segments. Set aside juice and segments. Season chicken with salt and pepper. Heat oil in pan and cook chicken for about 4-6 minutes on each side. Then take out and wrap in aluminium foil and let it cook in this for a little while. Add mustard, crème fraîche together with cornflour dissolved in orange juice to juices in pan, bring to the boil and season. Add the orange segments to the sauce. Unwrap chicken breasts and add any juices to the sauce. Serve chicken breasts with sauce poured over them. Serve with mashed potatoes and a green vegetable.

SPICY CHICKEN BAKED WITH GARLIC AND PAPRIKA

This dish has a lovely creamy garlicky sauce and takes very little time to prepare.

Serves 4.

4 medium chicken legs	1 tablespoon lemon juice
1 small onion, peeled and chopped	1 tablespoon oil
1 tablespoon paprika	1 tablespoon chopped thyme
2 tablespoons white wine vinegar	4 tablespoons low fat yoghurt
400g (14 oz) can chopped tomatoes	Salt and pepper
3 cloves garlic, peeled and chopped	

Arrange chicken in ovenproof dish. Fry onion in oil, then add the vinegar, tomatoes, chopped garlic, lemon juice, paprika and seasoning. Pour mixture over chicken and sprinkle with half the thyme. Cover with foil and cook for 50 minutes in preheated oven 180C, 350F, Gas Mark 4. Stir in the yoghurt just before serving and sprinkle over the remaining thyme and a little black pepper. This dish can be served with a salad or baked potatoes and carrots.

GRILLED HERBY AND GARLIC TURKEY BREASTS

You can use chicken for this recipe, and it makes an easy dish to serve in the summer when you don't want to spend too much time slaving over a hot stove.

Serves 4.

4 fairly thick turkey breasts	2 tablespoons lemon juice
4 garlic cloves, crushed	$\frac{1}{4}$ teaspoon salt
$\frac{1}{2}$ teaspoon dried thyme, rosemary and sage	$\frac{1}{4}$ teaspoon pepper
2 tablespoons olive oil	

Mix well together the garlic and herbs with the oil, lemon juice, salt and pepper. Brush this mixture over the slices of turkey and let stand in refrigerator for half an hour. Then grill under grill at highest temperature for 3 minutes on each side until cooked through. I usually serve this dish with fluffy boiled rice and sauté potatoes.

COLD SPICY CHICKEN

This recipe was given to me by an Australian friend and is definitely a dish to serve on a hot summer's day. It can be made the day before, and put into the refrigerator until required.

Serves 6.

2 1¼ kg (2 x 2lb 12oz) chickens (split in halves)
2 tablespoons coriander and fennel seeds
4 teaspoons ground cloves
4 tablespoons finely chopped ginger
1 teaspoon salt

4 cloves garlic finely chopped
Zest of 1 large lemon
2 green chillies (or to taste finely chopped)
100ml (4fl oz) olive oil

Roast the coriander and fennel seeds in a dry pan over a high heat until they darken. Grind them finely. Mix with all the other ingredients so that you have a thick paste, then rub paste all over the chicken halves. Marinate overnight or for about 5-6 hours. Preheat oven to 200C, 400F, Gas Mark 6 and put the chicken halves into a large roasting tin cut side down. Roast for about one hour basting from time to time until the chicken is tender. Cool completely and refrigerate. Serve with a green salad.

HONEY GARLIC AND LEMON CHICKEN

The honey, lemon and garlic give this chicken dish a delicious flavour, and cooking the potatoes with the chicken means that once it's in the oven it doesn't need much attention until it's cooked.

Serves 4-6.

3 lemons
50g 2oz butter
3 tablespoons clear honey
1 garlic clove, finely chopped

4 rosemary sprigs, leaves stripped from the stalks
8 chicken thighs or drumsticks
700g (1½ lb) potatoes, cut into small chunks

Cranberry and Apple Pie p86.

Bread and Butter Pudding p91.

Bread Pudding p93.

Raspberry and Almond Crumble p89.

Steamed Chocolate Pudding p91.

Poussins in Cider p42.

Kitchen
Utensils

Preheat oven to 200C, 400F, Gas Mark 6. Squeeze the juice from two lemons and put into a small pan with butter, honey, garlic, rosemary and plenty of salt and pepper. Heat gently until the butter melts. Arrange the chicken in one layer in a shallow roasting tin. Put the potatoes around the chicken. Drizzle the lemon, butter and honey mixture over the chicken and potatoes, turning potatoes over until everything is coated. Roast the chicken for 50 minutes to 1 hour, stirring a couple of times until the chicken is cooked and the potatoes are crisp and golden. Serve with a green salad or green beans.

ROAST DUCK WITH GREEN PEA STUFFING

Green peas are notably duck's most favoured complement, and it's so delicious it could quite easily suffice as a dish on its own, as well as being both light and economical, and it takes off the richness of the duck meat.

Serves 4.

1 young duckling 2kg (4½ lb) to 2¼ kg (5lb)	1 cup fresh brown breadcrumbs
3 medium onions, peeled & thinly sliced	2 medium eggs
2½ tablespoons butter	½ teaspoon each of salt and pepper
½ tablespoon brown sugar	450g (1lb) frozen peas
1 tablespoon chopped fresh mint	½ tablespoon finely grated orange zest

In a heavy pan sauté the onions slowly in the butter with the sugar added, stirring occasionally until soft and almost caramelised for about 20 minutes. Allow to cool, then add the mint, orange zest, breadcrumbs, egg, salt and pepper. Purée the frozen peas (which have been thawed slightly) and mix into the stuffing. Stuff into cleaned and dried duck cavity, then truss and tie duck with string. Season duck with salt and pepper, prick fatty parts then place in a large deep roasting tin or casserole. Pour over 2 cups of orange juice. Cover tightly with lid or tinfoil and roast at 180C, 350F, Gas Mark 4 for 2¼ hours. Remove lid and increase temperature to 200C, 400F, Gas Mark 6 to crisp the skin. Check bird from time to time so that the skin does not burn. When cooked pour off juices and fat and reserve juices for gravy.

ORANGE SAUCE GRAVY

This light fruity gravy is ideal to go with your roasted duck. It contains no fat and just a little cornflour to thicken.

Giblets & neck of duck
600ml (1 pint) water
A few stalks of parsley
2 tablespoons brown sugar
2 tablespoons malt vinegar
(or raspberry vinegar)

Salt and pepper to taste
Zest of ½ orange
½ tablespoon cornflour
2 tablespoons port
1 cup fresh orange juice

Simmer giblets with parsley in saucepan for about one hour, while ducks are cooking. In a separate saucepan place sugar and vinegar, and cook over medium heat for several minutes until mixture forms a light caramel. Strain liquid from giblets and add this to the saucepan, discarding the giblets. Simmer for 10 minutes and then add orange juice, salt and pepper and zest of orange. Mix cornflour with port and stir into sauce, allowing it to boil for a few minutes to cook cornflour (thicken to taste). This dish calls for roast potatoes, but as it is a rich dish, mashed potatoes go equally as well with green vegetables.

ROAST PHEASANT COOKED IN CIDER

Pheasant can tend to be on the dry side if it is roasted, so I think it's best to casserole it slowly in either wine or cider. The pheasant season is from 1st October until 31st January, and they are easily bought from most supermarkets. Pheasants can be cooked whole or jointed, but I prefer to cook mine whole.

Serves 4.

1 pheasant
1 onion, peeled and sliced
2 sticks celery, chopped
1 cooking apple, peeled, cored and chopped
225g (8 oz) mushrooms

2 tbsp plain flour, seasoned
300ml (½ pint) cider
35g (1½ oz) butter
300ml (½ pint) stock cube

Sprinkle the pheasant with the seasoned flour. Melt the butter and quickly fry the bird all over to seal juices. Remove the bird and lower the heat, add the onions and celery and cook for a few minutes, then add the mushrooms and apples and fry for a further 5 minutes. Strain off any surplus fat, add the cider and stock and bring to the boil. Return the pheasant to the pan or casserole dish, cover with lid and cook in preheated oven 180C,

350F, Gas Mark 4 for 1 – 1½ hours, until the meat is tender. Thicken the juices and serve as a separate gravy. Game chips go well with pheasant, but you can serve it with any vegetables of your choice.

DOUBLE CRUST RABBIT PIE

I make this pie at least two or three times a year and it's a great family favourite. Rabbits are easy to come by, and nowadays most supermarkets sell them already jointed, but I usually buy mine from my local butcher and get him to joint it for me.

Serves 4.

1 medium to large rabbit	1 clove garlic, finely chopped
175g (6 oz) streaky bacon, finely chopped	175g (6 oz) mushrooms
1 large onion, finely chopped	150ml (¼ pint) cider
175g (6 oz) mushrooms, sliced	½ teaspoon mustard powder
150ml (¼ pint) cider	1 level teaspoon grated nutmeg
25g (1 oz) butter	2 bay leaves and a sprig or two of thyme
25g (1 oz) flour	350g (12 oz) flaky or shortcrust pastry
Salt and pepper	1 beaten egg

Wash the rabbit and cut into about 8 pieces (or get your butcher to do this for you) and leave immersed in salt water (1 level teaspoon salt) for about two hours, then drain and rinse well. Put the rabbit together with all the seasoning, nutmeg, bay and thyme into a pan and all but cover with water. Simmer for 45 to 60 minutes. Leave to cool. Carefully remove meat from bone and cut all the flesh into smallish pieces. Strain the stock retaining ½ pint and add this to the cider to enhance the flavour. Melt the butter in a frying pan and add the onion, garlic and bacon. Cook for a few minutes stirring in the flour. Remove from heat and stir in stock a little at a time. Return to heat and, still stirring, bring to the boil and thicken the sauce. Remove from heat, add rabbit and mushrooms and more seasoning if required. Leave to cool. Roll out pastry to about 3mm (1/8 inch) thickness and line a pie dish. Damp the top edge all round, put in the filling and cover with a pastry lid, seal, trim and flute. Use the trimmings for decoration, then brush with the beaten egg, Bake for 20 minutes at 220C, 425F, Gas Mark 7 and then a further 20 minutes at 180C, 375F, Gas Mark 4. Serve with creamed potatoes and green vegetables.

PASTA DISHES AND SAUCES

This cook book would not be complete without a chapter on pasta! Most of us are familiar with Spaghetti Bolognaise – I remember it from my childhood days, winding the long wiggly worm-like strips around my fork. But now we have delicious sauces to accompany our pasta dishes, and when you're hard pressed for time a pasta meal is one that you can prepare and have ready to serve in a matter of minutes. I have an Italian friend who makes her own pasta, and there's nothing like homemade pasta but, having said that, there are so many kinds of pastas on the market now, all in different sizes and shapes, and which are as near as you will get to the homemade Italian variety. So in this chapter you will find a variety of pasta dishes with delicious sauces to accompany them.

Pasta Bows in Herb Dressing

SPAGHETTI WITH MUSHROOM SAUCE

A moist pasta dish with a light creamy sauce. Try a sprinkling of Parmesan cheese or nutmeg to give the pasta a piquant flavour.

Serves 4.

560g (1¼ lb) tiny mushrooms
2½ tablespoons oil
350g (12 oz) spaghetti
250ml (8floz) vegetable stock
Medium egg yolk

1½ teaspoons cornflour
1½ teaspoons French mustard
150g (5 oz) crème fraîche
Sprinkling of Parmesan cheese or
nutmeg

Cut mushrooms into thick slices and fry in heated oil. Then transfer onto vegetable stock and season to taste. Bring to the boil and simmer for about 5 minutes. Blend egg yolk with the cornflour and mustard, and gradually add the crème fraîche. Add to the mushroom mixture and thicken sauce by stirring continuously. Meanwhile cook the spaghetti following packet instructions. Pour sauce on to the drained spaghetti and add a sprinkling or Parmesan cheese or nutmeg, Serve immediately.

TAGLIATELLE PASTA WITH HAM AND MUSHROOMS

This dish is rather rich so you can replace the cream cheese with cottage cheese, which works just as well.

Serves 4.

450g (1lb) green tagliatelle
110g (4 oz) mushroom
25g (1 oz) butter
2 tablespoons flour
300ml (½ pint) chicken stock

350g (12 oz) ham
200g (7 oz) cream or cottage cheese
3 tablespoons parsley, chopped
Salt and pepper

Cook pasta in a large pan of boiling water as directed on packet (usually 12-15 minutes). Slice mushrooms and fry gently in melted butter for 3 minutes. Stir in the flour and cook, stirring for 1 minute. Gradually blend in stock and stir over moderate heat until thickened and smooth. Cut the ham into thin strips and add to the sauce with the cream or cottage cheese, pepper and parsley. Stir for about 3 minutes until well mixed and heated through. Drain the pasta thoroughly and serve topped with the sauce and a sprinkling of parsley.

BEEF AND ONION LASAGNE

This dish has a delicious rich flavour and freezes well. I sometimes make two and freeze one to have on hand when unexpected guests call.

Serves 4 (double ingredients for 8)

Meat Sauce:

350g 12 oz) extra lean minced beef
2 medium onions
6 button mushrooms
1 tablespoon tomato purée
1 tablespoon soy sauce
1 beef stock cube
3 tablespoon dry white wine
Salt and pepper
1 teaspoon dried marjoram

Cheese sauce:

225g (8 oz) curd cheese
3 eggs
75g (3 oz) grated Cheddar cheese

Pasta finish:

12 sheets oven ready lasagne verdi
2 tablespoons Parmesan cheese, grated

Cook beef on a very low heat until the juices run, gradually increasing heat. Finely chop onion and cut button mushrooms in half, then stir into beef with tomato purée, soy sauce, stock cube and wine. Bring to the boil, then reduce heat, cover and simmer for 20 – 25 minutes until mince is cooked. Season, stir in marjoram and cook for a further 5 minutes. Beat curd cheese and eggs together and stir in the grated Cheddar cheese. Layer lasagne sheets, beef sauce and cheese sauce in a lightly oiled oven proof dish, finishing off with the cheese sauce. Sprinkle with Parmesan cheese on top and bake in preheated oven 350F, 180C, Gas Mark 4 for 40 – 45 minutes until the top is golden brown and pasta is cooked.

EASY SPAGHETTI BOLOGNESE

An old favourite and one of the easiest dishes to make. I usually have most of the ingredients to hand in my cupboard, but vary the extra ingredients to suit what I can find!

Serves 4.

450g (1lb) minced beef
1 large onion, peeled and chopped
400g (14 oz) chopped tomatoes

2 tablespoons mixed dried herbs
Dried spaghetti – according to appetite
(I usually allow 75g (3oz) per serving)

3 tablespoons tomato purée

1 tablespoon vegetable oil

225g (8 oz) mushrooms, chopped

Heat oil in large pan and brown minced beef, chopped onion and mushrooms for 3-4 minutes. Add 3 tablespoons tomato purée, can of chopped tomatoes and 2 tablespoons mixed herbs. Bring to the boil and simmer for 20 minutes, stirring occasionally. Bring a large saucepan of slightly salted water to the boil, and then add spaghetti and cook for approximately 12 minutes, until firm to the bite. When spaghetti is ready, drain and return to pan, add sauce, stir and serve piping hot.

PASTA AĹ LA CLARA

This recipe was given to me by a friend and originally came from the Shoscombe School's 'Simply Delicious' Cookbook. The ingredients are easy to follow, as you can use as much as you like, according to the number of family or guests you are feeding!

1 large onion

1 garlic clove

Mushrooms (as many as you like)

Cheddar cheese (as much as you like)

Ham (as much as you like)

Tagliatelle (whole packet!)

400g (14 oz) tomato soup

1 tablespoon olive oil

You need to chop the onion, garlic, ham and mushrooms into small or thin pieces and grate the cheese. Heat the oil in large frying pan and fry the onion for 5 minutes, then add garlic to the pan together with the ham and mushrooms and add salt and pepper to taste. Meanwhile cook the tagliatelle according to the instructions on the packet, add the soup, cheese and tagliatelle and then mix all the ingredients together and serve.

PASTA SALAD

A deliciously cool and healthy salad to make on a hot summer's day, and it will keep well in refrigerator if you want to make it the day before.

Serves 4.

225g (8 oz) pasta shapes

Mint or chives, chopped

225g (8 oz) celery

2 tablespoons vegetable oil

450g (1lb) eating apples, diced

Dressing:

150g (5 oz) soured cream

2 tablespoons single cream

2 tablespoons lemon juice

2 tablespoons onion, chopped

2 tablespoons horseradish sauce

Salt and pepper

Cook pasta in plenty of salted boiling water for about 5 minutes. Drain and rinse well under cold, running water. Toss in the vegetable oil. Mix dressing ingredients and stir in apples, beetroot and celery. Leave in refrigerator until ready to serve. Then add pasta and garnish with mint or chives.

PASTA BOWS WITH GARLIC AND HERBS

Although I usually cook pasta bows in this recipe you can use any small pasta of your choice. Drizzle extra olive oil over the cooked pasta and it will keep until the next day, when it's delicious cold.

Serves 2 (double ingredients for 4)

110g (4 oz) pasta bows

2 cloves garlic

Mixed fresh chopped herbs of your choice

25g (1oz) butter

Sea Salt

Freshly ground black pepper

Cook pasta bows in plenty of salted, boiling water. While pasta is cooking chop garlic finely and fry in butter. Combine the cooked pasta, garlic and fresh chopped herbs together and season with salt and pepper.

PASTA WITH SPICY CHICKEN

This recipe came from the Friends of Boxford School. With the chilli and other flavourings coming through the dish it makes a satisfying meal which is full of flavour.

Serves 4

1 teaspoon chilli powder

Pinch of cayenne

1 400g (14 oz) tin tomatoes

1½ tablespoons olive oil

1 onion, peeled and chopped

1 teaspoon turmeric

Fresh basil

1 teaspoon sugar

250g (8 oz) skinned chicken breasts cut into   350g (12 oz) dried pasta, penne or fusilli
small pieces

Mix the chilli, cayenne, turmeric with 1 teaspoon of olive oil in a bowl to form a paste.
Add the chicken pieces, mix thoroughly, cover and set aside for 15 minutes. Heat the
remaining oil in a pan and fry the onion until soft. Add the tin of tomatoes, sugar and
some finely chopped basil (save some for the garnish). Bring to the boil, stirring
occasionally, then leave to simmer. Cook the pasta for 8-10 minutes until just tender. Dry
fry the chicken pieces in a non-stick pan for about 10 minutes, then add to the tomato
sauce. Drain the pasta, drizzle with a little olive oil and add seasoning to taste. Arrange
pasta in a serving dish and pour over the sauce. Serve garnished with the remaining basil.

BUTTERFLY PASTA WITH MARSALA

**From time to time I do get recipes sent in to me, and this one came from the
Marsala Wine people. Adding the Marsala wine gives this dish a delicious
piquant taste.**

Serves 3-4.

400g (14 oz) butterfly pasta (dry)   1 onion
½ glass of Marsala   1 tablespoon flour
2 tablespoons of butter or olive oil   Salt and black pepper
225ml (8 fl oz) vegetable stock (or stock cube)

Mix the stock and flour together. Peel and chop the onion finely and gently fry in the
butter or oil. When cooked add the flour/stock mixture. Lower the heat and simmer until
the sauce has thickened. Add the Marsala and season to taste, then simmer until reduced
slightly. As soon as the sauce starts to boil remove from heat and set aside. Boil the pasta
in the usual way, and when it has cooked pour over the Marsala sauce. Grate black pepper
over the top and serve immediately.

SPAGHETTI WITH BROCCOLI AND CHEESE

**I've used blue cheese in this recipe to give it a 'bite' but if you prefer a milder
cheese it will work just as well.**

Serves 4.

350g (12 oz) spaghetti

450g (1lb) broccoli, cut into small florets

1 tablespoon olive oil

110g (2 oz) mixed chopped nuts

Salt and pepper

2 garlic cloves, finely chopped

4 tablespoons fresh chopped parsley

Grated rind and juice of 1 small lemon

110g (4 oz) blue cheese, crumbled

Cook the pasta in a pan of boiling water, following instructions on the packet. Add the broccoli for the last 3 minutes of cooking time. Heat a little oil in a small pan, add the nuts and cook until lightly toasted, stirring to keep from burning. Add garlic and cook for about 20 seconds until just brown. Remove from heat and stir in the parsley and lemon rind. Drain the pasta and broccoli, then return to the pan and stir in the nut mixture and cheese. Season, then drizzle with some oil and lemon juice.

PASTA AĹ SALMON

This pasta dish makes a delicious and unusual starter, or you could serve it for a light lunch or supper.

Serves 4-6.

3 tablespoons unsalted butter

75g (3 oz) smoked salmon, cut into small strips

1 tablespoon peeled, chopped shallots or spring onions

Juice of ½ a lemon

300ml (½ pint) double cream

2 tablespoons Scotch whisky

350g (12 oz) dried penne pasta

Salt and black pepper

Melt butter in large frying pan over a low heat and cook the shallots for about 2 minutes. Put the pasta in boiling, salted water and cook until it is just al denté. Add the lemon juice to the cooked shallots and mix well. Stir in the cream and whisky, raising the heat just long enough to let the alcohol evaporate. Add salt and pepper and stir well. Drain the pasta, and gently combine the pasta and the sauce, which should be smooth and creamy. Add a little more cream if the sauce is too dry. Then quickly stir in the smoked salmon before serving with freshly ground black pepper on top.

SPINACH CANNELLONI

A delicious creamy sauce dish which is good to eat at lunch or supper times. It's quite low in calories too if you use reduced fat cheeses.

Serves 4.

8 cannelloni tubes

3 small tomatoes

110g (4 oz) baby spinach leaves

1 teaspoonful oil 25g (1 oz) pine nuts (optional)

Freshly ground black pepper

Freshly chopped parsley

50g (2 oz) reduced fat Cheddar cheese, grated

Make up 850ml (1½ pints) cheese sauce or buy 525g (carton ready-made) sauce

Sprinkling of paprika

75g (3 oz) breadcrumbs

150g (5 oz) reduced fat soft cheese with garlic and herbs

Cook cannelloni in lightly salted boiling water for 6-8 minutes, drain and set aside. Finely chop tomatoes and shred spinach. Heat oil in pan and sauté the spinach for 2-3 minutes until it wilts. Add tomatoes, nuts, half the breadcrumbs and the soft cheese and heat for a few minutes so that all the ingredients are well mixed. Season with black pepper. Cool slightly and fill tubes. Transfer the cannelloni to oven proof dish and pour over the made-up or ready-made cheese sauce. Sprinkle with the grated Cheddar cheese and remaining breadcrumbs. Bake in preheated oven 190C, 375F, Gas Mark 5 for 35-40 minutes until golden brown. Serve sprinkled with parsley and paprika.

WALNUT PASTA SAUCE

This is a quick and easy sauce to make, which was given to me by an Australian friend. I find that it goes well with spaghetti and makes a change from the usual bolognese sauce.

Makes 5-6 servings.

¼ cup of olive oil

1 teaspoon crushed garlic

1½ cups finely chopped walnuts

½ cup grated parmesan cheese

½ coarse black pepper

1 tablespoon fresh chopped thyme

2 tablespoons chopped parsley

2 tablespoons capers

Salt to taste

Sauté the garlic in heated oil for 30 seconds. Add the walnuts and toss over heat for about 1 minute. Add the cream and bring to the boil. Remove from the heat and mix in the cheese and seasonings. Season to taste with salt. Toss through the cooked pasta until it is well coated and ready to serve.

SPEEDY TOMATO SAUCE

This sauce can be made in 20 minutes. I always make a large quantity as it freezes well and can be kept in the freezer to have on hand when required.

Makes 4 - 6 servings.

400g (14 oz) tin tomatoes

2 tablespoons vinegar

2 medium onions, peeled and chopped

10g ($\frac{1}{2}$ oz) butter

2 teaspoons cornflour

25g (1 oz) ham

Salt and pepper

Melt butter and fry ham and chopped onions until softened, add the vinegar and tomatoes and simmer for 15 minutes. Purée in liquidiser and then return to heat and thicken with cornflour.

SHRIMP SAUCE

A colourful sauce which goes well with pasta and will surprise your guests when you serve it!

Makes about 4 generous servings.

600ml (1 pint)

300ml ($\frac{1}{2}$ pint) shrimps

50g (2 oz) butter

35g ($1\frac{1}{2}$ oz) flour

4 teaspoons anchovy sauce

$\frac{1}{2}$ teaspoon cayenne pepper

Wash and skin shrimps. Melt the butter and add the flour and stock. Bring to the boil stirring constantly, and then simmer for 3 minutes. Add anchovy sauce, shrimps and cayenne, and liquidise in liquidiser.

BASIL SAUCE

Using basil and pine nuts with the two cheeses blended together make a rich green sauce which will accompany any pasta of your choice.

Serves 6.

3 tablespoons freshly grated Parmesan cheese
2 tablespoons freshly grated Romano cheese
(or goats cheese)
30g (1 oz) pine nuts

2 cloves garlic
120ml (4floz) olive oil
35g (1½ oz) fresh basil (or dried)

In a blender or food processor, combine the basil with salt to taste until chopped. Add the cheeses, pine nuts, garlic and olive oil and process until smooth and creamy. Leave the mixture in the blender, and add one tablespoon of the pasta cooking water to the basil mixture and process again. Serve on hot pasta.

VEGETABLE DISHES

Vegetables play an important part in our diet and in this chapter I have tried to give recipes that are nutritious but can stand alone as main meals, as well as a side accompaniment to a main dish as well. Unless I am using vegetables with other ingredients I always steam them, as minerals and vitamins C and B are water soluble and are lost by seepage into cooking water and even in the water in which vegetables are steamed. So raw and lightly cooked vegetables will provide the best nutritional value and source of fibre, and any cooking liquid should, if possible, be used in stocks, gravies or sauces.

Glazed Carrots and Beans

ASPARAGUS AND PEPPER MILLE FEUILLES

When asparagus is in season this is a delightful colourful dish to make, and as most of us use ready-made puff pastry these days, it doesn't take long to assemble and cook.

Serves 4-6

Cheese Sauce:

110g (4 oz) ready-made puff pastry

110g (4 oz) fresh asparagus

50g (2 oz) mushrooms, sliced

2 teaspoons oil

175g (6 oz) mixed peppers, sliced in a little oil

2 tablespoons Parmesan cheese

1 tablespoon chopped parsley

25g (1 oz) low fat spread

2 level tablespoons plain flour

200ml (7 fl oz) semi-skimmed milk

50g (2 oz) matured reduced-fat Cheddar cheese, grated

Freshly ground black pepper

Divide pastry into three and roll out each piece to a rectangle 25x10cm (10"x4"). Place on a foil-covered tray and prick all over with a fork and bake in preheated oven 230C, 450F, Gas Mark 8 for about 10 minutes. Then set aside and make sauce. Combine spread, flour and milk in a pan and heat until spread has melted. Bring to the boil, whisking all the time, then remove from heat and add cheese and season to taste. Blanch asparagus for a 2-3 minutes, drain well and cut into small pieces. Cook sliced mushrooms in a little oil and stir into the peppers with the asparagus, and heat through. Spread a thin layer of cheese sauce over one sheet of pastry and add half the vegetables evenly. Top with a little more cheese sauce and place another layer of pastry on top; repeat layers and top with the final sheet of pastry. Serve sprinkled with Parmesan cheese and freshly chopped parsley.

POTATO RÖSTI

I like to serve this potato dish with fish or, as an accompaniment to a roast or chicken dish. It also makes a satisfying lunch meal with a poached egg on top of one of the rösti. Allow at least 2 portions per serving.

Serves 4.

565g (1¼lb) large baking potatoes

2 tablespoons oil

1 tablespoon freshly chopped coriander

1 medium onion, peeled and chopped

Salt and freshly ground black pepper

Clean and prick the potatoes over with a fork and bake at 200C, 400F, Gas Mark 6 for 40-45 minutes, until softened, but not cooked through. Heat oil in pan and sauté onion until golden. Cool potatoes then peel and grate coarsely. Then stir in onion with the coriander. Season well. Spoon 8 mounds onto a well greased baking tray and bake in preheated oven 200C, 400F, Gas Mark 6 for 45 minutes until golden and crisp. Garnish with chopped coriander.

SPECIAL BRUSSEL SPROUTS WITH HERBS

Guaranteed to convert those who do not like Brussels sprouts, even small children will enjoy the taste and dressed up look of this vegetable when it is served.

Serves 4-6

1kg (2¼ lb) Brussels sprouts
10g (½ oz) fresh parsley, chopped
10g (½ oz) fresh basil
150ml (5fl oz) tub crème fraîche
10g (½ oz) fresh chives, chopped
200ml (7fl oz) skimmed milk

40g (1½ oz) butter
40g (1½ oz) plain flour
Pinch of grated nutmeg
40g (1½ oz) hazelnuts, chopped
Seasoning to taste

Cook Brussels in lightly salted water for 5-6 minutes until tender. Combine butter, flour and milk in a large saucepan and bring almost to the boil, whisking until thickened. Stir in crème fraîche and warm through. Remove from the heat and add the herbs, nutmeg and seasoning, stirring gently. Drain sprouts and spoon into a dish and pour sauce over. Sprinkle with nuts and grill under preheated grill on high for 3 minutes until bubbling and piping hot.

LEMONY ROASTED POTATOES

I find these roasted potatoes with a lemony flavour go well with pork or chicken and provides a sharp taste to absorb the richness of the meat.

Serves 4-6.

1 kg (2¼ lb) new potatoes, washed
4 tablespoonfuls olive oil
Grated rind of 2 lemons
Juice of 2 lemons

1½ teaspoons sugar
Salt and pepper to taste
Chives

Cook the potatoes in lightly salted water for about 6 minutes. Drain and place in a roasting tin, adding olive oil, lemon rind and lemon juice, sugar and salt and pepper, and combine together. Roast in preheated oven 190C, 375F, Gas Mark 5 for 25-30 minutes, stir and baste often. Serve with some chopped chives sprinkled over the potatoes.

SWEET POTATO AND BRUSSELS SPROUT PATTIES

These little patties make a delicious light lunch served with a green salad and sour cream, they will also freeze well too.

Serves 4.

225g (8 oz) Brussels sprouts, cleaned and trimmed
450g (1lb) potatoes, chopped in chunks
225g (8oz) brown-skinned sweet potatoes, roughly chopped
25g (1 oz) butter
1 tablespoon olive oil

2 teaspoons ground coriander
Small bunch fresh coriander, chopped
1 tablespoonful flour
Vegetable oil
1 medium onion, peeled and sliced
3 garlic cloves, peeled and crushed

Cook the sprouts in lightly salted boiling water for 6-7 minutes until tender. Drain sprouts and cool, then shred. Add the potatoes and sweet potatoes to the boiling water and cook for 7-8 minutes until tender. Heat butter and oil in large frying pan, then add the onion and garlic and cook for 4-5 minutes. Sprinkle over the ground coriander and cook for about 1 minute. Drain and mash the potatoes. In a bowl mix the sprouts, mashed potatoes, fresh coriander and onion mixture. Season. Shape into eight patties and coat in flour. Heat vegetable oil in frying pan and fry the patties for 4-5 minutes each side until golden. Serve hot with salad.

GLAZED GREEN BEANS

This recipe is popular in America and was given to me by an American friend when we lived in Somerset. We had glut of French beans and this was one way of using them up.

Serves 10 (but you can halve the amount of ingredients for less)

1 tablespoon vegetable oil
$2\frac{1}{2}$ cups red onion, peeled and sliced
900g (2 lb) green beans, trimmed
$\frac{1}{2}$ cup water

$\frac{1}{4}$ cup soy sauce
$1\frac{1}{2}$ tablespoons sugar
3 tablespoons rice vinegar

Heat oil in a large non-stick pan over medium heat. Add onion and stir fry 1 minute.
Increase heat to medium high. Add beans and stir fry for 1 minute. Stir in water and
remaining ingredients and bring to the boil. Cover, reduce heat and simmer for 12 minutes until tender. Uncover and bring to a boil and cook for 10 minutes until liquid almost
evaporates. Toss gently to combine.

COURGETTES AND ONIONS

**An easy side dish to cook which goes with almost any main meal. I find it will
heat up well, if you have any left over.**

450g (1lb) green courgettes
1 fairly large onion, peeled and sliced
Generous knob of butter

Pinch of salt
Freshly ground black pepper

Wash and top and tail courgettes and slice them into a greased oven dish. Add the sliced
onion and combine with the courgette slices. Add a knob of butter, a pinch of salt and a
generous sprinkle of freshly ground black pepper. Cook in preheated oven 190C. 375F,
Gas Mark 5 for about 35-45 minutes. Drain well before serving`

VEGETABLE PASTIES

**These small pasties are ideal to take on a picnic and eaten cold, or eaten
straight from the oven with a green salad for lunch.**

Serves 4.

450g (1lb) puff pastry
1 egg, beaten

For the filling:

50ml (2fl oz) vegetable stock
2 teaspoons dried thyme
2 tablespoons tomato purée
Seasoning to taste
1 large carrot, diced
1 large potato, diced

1 small parsnip, diced
½ small celeriac, grated
25g (1 oz) butter
1 large onion, peeled and chopped
1 garlic clove, crushed

Roll out pastry on floured surface into a fairly large thin rectangle, then cut out four rounds of pastry about 18cm (7 inches) use a plate as a guide. Then set aside. Melt butter in pan, add onion, garlic, potato, carrot, parsnip and celeriac and fry for about 8-10 minutes. Add the stock, cover and simmer over lowered heat for 10 minutes until the vegetables are tender. Combine vegetables, thyme and tomato purée and seasoning into a bowl. When mixture has cooled spoon a quarter of it into the centre of each pastry round. Dampen the edges and draw up to form pasties. Put pasties onto baking sheet and flute up the edges with a knife, then brush with beaten egg. Bake in preheated oven 200C, 400F, Gas Mark 6 for 25-30 minutes until pasties are golden brown.

STUFFED COURGETTES AND TOMATOES

These stuffed courgettes make an excellent starter to a main course. Allow two courgette cases per person as the filling is quite substantial.

Serves 4.

4 fairly large courgettes
1 heaped tablespoon Gruyere or
Emmenthal cheese
2 tablespoons fine, white breadcrumbs

A little garlic butter
3 garlic cloves, crushed
Salt and pepper to season

Garlic butter: Cream 110g (4 oz) butter and add 2-3 crushed garlic cloves and 2 heaped tablespoons fresh parsley, and add 1 flat teaspoon salt. Beat together and store in an air-tight plastic container and use as required.

Steam courgettes until tender but firm, about 12 minutes. Then split lengthwise and fork out filling from courgette and mash to a pulp. Mix in the breadcrumbs, cheese and bind with a little garlic butter. Salt and pepper to season, then put mixture into courgette cases. Brush tops with oil and bake in preheated oven 190C, 375F, Gas Mark 5 for about 15 minutes, until filling is cooked through.

Stuffed tomatoes can be made in the same way as above. You will need 4 firm fairly large tomatoes: Halve the tomatoes between top and base (not downwards), scoop out filling and mix with 1 small teacup soft, brown breadcrumbs, 1 flat dessertspoon chopped chives, parsley and tarragon. Mix with a little garlic butter, salt and pepper, drizzle a little oil over the tops and bake in preheated oven 190C, 375F, Gas Mark 5 for about 15 minutes.

STUFFED ONIONS WITH SAVOURY MEAT FILLING

This is one of my favourite ways of serving onions, especially the large Spanish ones. I very often serve them as a main dish with vegetables.

Serves 3-4.

6 large Spanish onions, peeled   A little oil
Sprigs of rosemary to garnish

Meat filling:

Cooked cores of the 6 Spanish onions   1 dessertspoon tomato purée
110g (4 oz) cold cooked minced beef   1 egg yolk
1 teaspoon finely chopped thyme   Salt and pepper

Place onions in a pan of salted, boiling water and simmer until tender. Remove, drain and cool. Remove centres of each onion carefully and set aside. Place all ingredients in a large bowl, together with the cooked onion cores, and mix thoroughly. Fill meat filling into the onion shells. Place in a baking tin, brush each onion lightly with oil, cover with foil and bake in preheated oven 180C, 350F, Gas Mark 4 for 15-20 minutes. Serve with Italian meat sauce as given below.

ITALIAN MEAT SAUCE

225g (8 oz) minced beef   425ml (15fl oz) beef stock (or cube)
1 large onion   1 medium carrot
1 tablespoon flour   1 stalk of celery
110g (4 oz) mushrooms   1 dessertspoon chopped parsley
1 teaspoon tomato purée   10g (½ oz) butter
90ml (3fl oz) dry white wine   10g (½ oz) olive oil
Salt and pepper to season

Finely dice the onion, carrot, celery and mushrooms. Heat oil and butter together in large frying pan and fry onion for about 1 minute, add carrot, parsley, celery and mushrooms and cook gently for 4-5 minutes. Add in the meat, working in thoroughly until mixture is brown all over. Add flour, and combine in tomato purée, adding the wine gradually and then the 425ml (15fl oz) stock. Season to taste and simmer, stirring occasionally and, if mixture seems too thick, add more stock.

POTATO CAKE

When the new potatoes have made way for the 'old ones' then this is a dish to cook. Easy to assemble and heats up well.

Serves 4.

450g (1lb), cooked, sieved, old potatoes

3 eggs separated

25g (1oz) butter

Salt and pepper to season

Turn cooked, sieved potatoes into a large bowl and beat in the 3 eggs yolks and 25g (1 oz) butter while potato mixture is still hot. Season to taste with salt and pepper. Whip up egg whites stiffly and beat into potato mixture. Turn mixture into lightly buttered dish and bake in preheated oven 200C, 400F, Gas Mark 6 for 25 minutes until mixture has risen and the top is golden brown.

STEAMED SUMMER VEGETABLES

Yellow and green courgettes make a colourful dish, but you can use any vegetables of your choice.

Serves 4-6.

675g (1½ lb) mixed yellow and green baby courgettes, baby carrots, young peas and flat beans

4 tablespoons olive oil

2 tablespoons fresh herbs, chives, tarragon, basil and rosemary

Seasoning

Steam vegetables separately until tender. Transfer to a warmed serving dish and mix in chopped herbs. Add olive oil and season to taste. Serve immediately.

VEGETARIAN

Although I am not a vegetarian, I find it useful to use up what root vegetables and pulses that are near their sell-by date lying around in my store cupboard, and with the variety of other vegetables we are able to buy nowadays it's fun to try out dishes that are completely meatless and a change from the usual meat and two veg. meals that are often on our menus. The recipes I have given in this chapter will appeal, I hope, to non-vegetarians as well as to the bona fide ones, as they are not only healthy and low in fat, but will help you to slim too!

Chestnut and Stilton Pie

MUSHROOM AND AUBERGINE FLAN

This flan is delicious eaten hot or cold and is ideal to take on a picnic, and you can make into individual flans which are easier to freeze and take out one at a time if you don't need a whole flan.

Serves 4.

Pastry:

175g (6oz) plain flour
75g (3 oz) butter
5 teaspoons cold water

Filling:

1 medium aubergine
75g (3 oz) mushrooms sliced
1 tbsp olive oil
1 small onion, chopped
2 medium eggs, beaten
1 garlic clove, crushed
150ml (¼ pint) milk
½ teaspoon dried oregano
Salt

Add salt to flour, then rub in the fats until the mixture resembles breadcrumbs. Add enough water to bind mixture together and rest pastry in refrigeration for about 25 minutes. Roll out pastry and line a 20cm (8") flan tin or ring. Slice aubergine, sprinkle with a little salt and leave for about 25 minutes. Rinse and pat dry. Heat tablespoon olive oil in pan and fry onion and garlic for 5 minutes. Put into flan case, then fry aubergine slices. Drain well and place in flan. Add sliced mushrooms on top of mixture in flan. Add oregano to the beaten eggs and pour over flan. Bake in pre-heated oven 200C, 400F, Gas Mark 6 for about 30 minutes, until set and golden brown.

POTATO, LEEK AND CHEDDAR CHEESE GRATIN

Cheddar cheese is a well flavoured cheese that gives a dish a piquancy that lingers on the taste buds. I've used cream in this recipe because it gives the dish a smooth substance.

Serves 4-6.

1.25kg (2½ lb) fairly large potatoes cut
into thick slices

1 tablespoon fresh sage leaves, chopped
225g (8 oz) vegetarian Cheddar, grated

3 tablespoons sunflour oil
450g (1lb) leeks, cleaned and sliced
300ml (½ pint) cider

Salt and pepper to taste
300ml (½ pint) double cream
Seasoning

Pre-heat oven to 190C, 375F, Gas Mark 5. Cook potatoes in boiling water for about 15 minutes. Drain and set aside. Heat oil in large pan and gently cook leeks for about 5 minutes until softened. Add the cider and bring to the boil until the liquid is reduced by about two-thirds. Stir in the cream and bring back to the boil, then remove from heat. Add sage and season to taste. Place one-third of the cream mixture and half the potatoes and seasoning in a large baking dish, then top with another one third of the cream mixture and sprinkle over half the grated cheese and the remaining potatoes and season again. Finish with a layer of the cream mixture, then sprinkle over the remaining cheese. Bake for 1¼ hours until golden and bubbling hot.

Serve with steamed cabbage.

LEEK AND PARSNIP HONEY GLAZED TART

My family ask for this tart time and time again, so I always try to make two and then have one spare in the freezer.

Serves 4.

Pastry:

For the topping:

175g (6 oz) plain flour
½ teaspoon salt
Generous pinch of Cayenne pepper
75g (3 oz) butter
25g (1 oz) vegetarian Parmesan, freshly grated

3 tbsp olive oil
450g (1lb) parsnips, thickly sliced
1 large leek, thickly sliced
1 tablespoon honey
1 tablespoon red wine vinegar
Seasoning

Sift flour, salt and cayenne into a mixing bowl and rub in the butter until the mixture resembles breadcrumbs. Add the Parmesan and mix to a stiff dough adding 2-3 tablespoons cold water. Knead into a ball and leave to chill in refrigerator while you are making the topping. Pre-heat oven to 200C, 400F, Gas Mark 6. Heat the oil in a deep flameproof gratin dish. Arrange parsnips and leeks in single layer in the bottom of dish and spoon over the honey, vinegar and seasoning. Cook gently for about 15 minutes until the parsnips are golden brown and almost cooked through. Remove from the heat. Roll out the pastry to a circle the same diameter as the dish (about 23cm 9") and lift over the vegetables and press into place. Put into oven and cook for 25 minutes or until the pastry is cooked through and golden. Remove the tart from the oven and leave to stand for 5 minutes, then turn onto a serving plate so that the vegetables are on the top. Can be served warm or cold.

VEGETABLE CURRY

This is a tasty colourful dish and is very low in calories. I usually use whatever vegetables I have to hand, and it takes less than hour to prepare and be ready to serve at table.

Serves 4.

2 tablespoons vegetable oil	1 teaspoon chilli powder
1 medium onion, peeled and chopped	2 teaspoons ground coriander
450g (1lb) mixed vegetables, diced, (carrots,	½ teaspoonful turmeric
peas, red kidney beans and potatoes)	Salt
3 tomatoes, skinned and chopped	

Heat oil in large pan and gently fry the onion until golden. Add the diced vegetables and stir in the chilli powder, coriander, turmeric and salt to taste. Then add the tomatoes and 2 tablespoons water, stir well and cover and cook gently for about 12 minutes until the juices have reduced and the mixture is almost dry.

LEEK & POTATO HASH

This is a very easy dish which is quick to make. Served with a poached egg on each portion it makes a substantial supper dish or a light lunch.

Serves 4.

4 large potatoes, baked in their jackets	25g (1 oz) butter
2 medium onions, peeled and sliced	1 tablespoons vegetable oil
4 medium leeks, cut into 2.5cm (1") pieces	Salt and pepper to taste
4 eggs	

When potatoes are cooked and cool, peel and shred them, discarding the skins. Melt the butter in a pan and fry the onion and leeks for about 6 minutes until they are soft and lightly brown. Mix the onion and leeks with the potatoes and season the mixture well. Heat oil in a large frying pan and when it's hot, spoon the hash mixture into the pan covering most of the pan. When the hash is lightly brown and crunchy lift out on to a dish first loosening with a spatula or slice, place a dish over the pan and then turn upside down so the hash slides on to the plate. While the hash is cooking you can poach your eggs for about 3 minutes, drain and then place each egg on a portion of hash.

NUTTY POTATO CRUMBLE

This is a dish that can be prepared well in advance and heated up for supper or lunch. For those allergic to nuts, please note that this recipe contains hazelnuts.

Serves 4-6.

450g (1lb) potatoes	300ml (½ pint) cheese sauce
2 eggs	75g (3 oz) hazelnuts
1 medium onion, peeled and chopped	110g (4 oz) granary breadcrumbs
110g (4 oz) green cabbage	50g (2 oz) Low fat Cheddar cheese
50g (2 oz) butter	Salt and black pepper

Hard boil the eggs. Peel and thickly slice the potatoes and boil for about 5 minutes, then drain and set aside. Wash and shred the cabbage. Heat about 25g (1 oz) vegetable oil in large pan and lightly fry cabbage and chopped onion. Arrange potatoes, cabbage, onion and chopped eggs in a greased ovenproof dish and season well. Mix up cheese sauce and pour over vegetables. Then mix roughly chopped hazelnuts, butter and breadcrumbs and sprinkle over vegetables. Top with the grated Cheddar cheese. Bake in preheated oven 180C, 350F, Gas Mark 4 for 45 minutes or until nicely golden and vegetables are cooked through, taking care that top doesn't brown too quickly.

CRUNCHY POTATO PIE

This dish has generous proportions, so halve the ingredients if you want to serve 4 instead of the 8 I have given in this recipe. It reheats well so you can make it the day before it's required.

Serves 8.

1kg (2¼ lb) potatoes, peeled and sliced very thickly	Freshly ground black pepper
	½ teaspoon dried oregano
2 medium onions, peeled and sliced thinly	200g (7 oz) gruyère cheese, grated
¼ cup olive oil	2 tablespoons fresh white breadcrumbs
½ cup tinned tomatoes, drained and mashed	¾ teaspoon salt

Grease ovenproof dish with oil and cover base and sides with a layer of potatoes (about a quarter of them) and scatter over a third of the onions. Drizzle over a little oil and a third of the tomatoes, season with salt and pepper and oregano. Scatter over a quarter of the cheese. Repeat layers ending with a layer of potatoes then cheese. Sprinkle over the breadcrumbs and a little oil, then cover with tinfoil. Bake in preheated oven 200C, 400F, Gas Mark 6 for 30 minutes, then remove foil and bake for a further 45 minutes until cooked and really golden on top.

WINTER CASSEROLE

Using French prunes in this recipe gives a delicious flavour and served with steamed cabbage it makes a substantial winter meal.

Serves 4.

225g (8 oz) baby or pickling onions
2 tablespoons vegetable oil
2 garlic cloves, crushed (optional)
4 medium carrots, peeled and thickly sliced
2 medium parsnips, peeled and thickly sliced
225g (8 oz) celeriac, peeled and cut into
thick chunks
225g (8 oz) swede, peeled and cut into chunks
4 tablespoons of sherry

300ml (½ pint) red wine
400ml (14 floz) vegetable stock
1 tablespoon tomato purée
1 fresh bouquet garni
225g (8 oz) French prunes
3 small leeks, cleaned and sliced
2 tablespoons cornflour, blended with
cold water to make a smooth paste
Salt and black pepper

Place the onions in a bowl and pour boiling water over them. Leave for 5 minutes, then drain. Use a small knife to help slip the skins off and cut in half. Heat the oil in a large pan and fry the onions for 5 minutes until softened. Stir in the garlic, sliced carrots and parsnips, chunks of celeriac and swede and fry for a further 4 minutes. Stir in the sherry, red wine, stock, tomato purée and bouquet garni into the pan and bring mixture to the boil, cover and simmer gently for 30 minutes, stirring from time to time. Add the prunes and leeks and simmer for a further 10-15 minutes. Stir in the cornflour mixture and gently simmer for a further 2-3 minutes, stirring continuously until the sauce is thickened and smooth. Season to taste.

LEEK AND ONION YORKSHIRE PUDDING

A friend of mine loves Yorkshire Pudding, but doesn't eat meat, so I devised this one for her. You can use spring onions and thinly sliced carrots as an alternative which tastes just as good. Served with roasted red and green peppers and a thick onion gravy - I guarantee you won't even miss the roast beef!

Serves 4.

3 tablespoons olive oil

450g (1lb) shallots

2 leeks, thickly sliced

4 large mushrooms, peeled and thinly sliced

For the batter:

110g (4 oz) plain flour

¼ teaspoon mustard powder

¼ teaspoon salt

1 egg, beaten

300ml (½ pint) semi-skimmed milk

and water mixed

Pour oil into a small roasting tin and put into preheated oven 220C, 425F, Gas Mark 7, and add shallots, leeks and mushrooms and sprinkle with sugar, and cook on hob over a medium heat for 10-15 minutes. Then make batter. Sift the flour, salt and mustard into a mixing bowl, make a well in the centre and add beaten egg and then gradually beat in the milk and water, adding the flour to make a smooth batter. Pour over the vegetables and cook in preheated oven 220C, 425F, Gas Mark 7 for about 45 minutes. Serve immediately with a thick onion gravy and roasted red and green peppers, or any root vegetables of your choice.

VEGETARIAN NUT ROAST

A tasty dish which, surprisingly, has plenty of flavour, and freezes well too. Serve hot with jacket potatoes, tomatoes, carrots or peas.

Serves 3-4.

110g (4 oz) peanuts, minced

Knob of butter

½ an onion, peeled and chopped

Tomato ketchup

1 tablespoon water from potatoes

1 cup mashed potatoes

1 cup brown breadcrumbs

1 egg

Salt and pepper

Fry peanuts and onion in butter to brown. Add potatoes and bread crumbs, beaten egg, tomato ketchup and potato water. Stir well and place in a flat tin. Dot with pats of butter and cook in preheated oven 180C, 350F, Gas Mark 4 for about 30 minutes.

SPRING ONION AND PARSLEY FLAN IN WALNUT PASTRY

Try to make the pastry well in advance and rest in refrigerator, it will be easier to handle and will have a firm crisp texture when it is baked.

Serves 4.

For the pastry:

175g (6 oz) butter or margarine

1 medium egg

Pinch of salt

150g (5 oz) plain flour

110g (4 oz) ground walnuts

For the filling:

4 small eggs

175ml (6 floz) skimmed milk

175ml (6 floz) double cream

1 tablespoon chopped parsley

6 spring onions, chopped

Grated nutmeg to taste

Seasoning

Make pastry, mixing together butter and egg with pinch of salt, then stir in the flour and ground walnuts. Knead all ingredients well and leave in refrigerator for 30 minutes. To make filling whisk together all ingredients. Then roll out pastry and line a greased 25cm (10 in) flan tin. Bake blind in preheated oven for 15 minutes. Pour the filling into the pastry case and bake for a further 30 minutes, until the top is golden brown and the filling set. Serve warm with a green salad.

RED LENTIL AND AUBERGINE RATATOUILLE

The red lentils and herbs used in this recipe make a colourful and deliciously flavoured casserole dish.

Serves 4.

450g (1lb) aubergines

2 medium onions, 225g

1 large red pepper

1 large green pepper

2 cloves garlic

3 tablespoons olive oil

2 small sprigs of rosemary

2 teaspoons chopped thyme

400g (14 oz) can chopped tomatoes

225g (8 oz) courgettes

225g (8 oz) red lentils

600ml (1 pint) vegetable stock

Salt and pepper

Cube the aubergines and put into a colander and sprinkle with salt. Leave for 30 minutes, then rinse well and pat dry. Peel onions and coarsely chop, slice courgettes and cut the red and green pepper into pieces and then crush cloves of garlic. Heat oil in a large casserole dish and fry the aubergines, onions, courgettes and garlic for 3-4 minutes until beginning to soften. Add the pepper and stir-fry for 1 minute. Add rosemary leaves to pan with thyme and tomatoes in juice, then bring to the boil. Add the red lentils and half the vegetable stock. Then cover and simmer for 15 minutes, adding more stock as necessary. Season to taste and serve piping hot with crusty bread or rolls.

SALADS AND DRESSINGS

With so much fresh produce we can buy in the shops today we're spoilt for choice when it comes to salads. When I was a child a salad usually consisted of lettuce, tomato, cucumber and, if you were lucky, spring onions. But today there is a whole variety to choose from, such as red and green peppers, baby new potatoes, bean sprouts, diced courgettes, and a host of other ingredients which you will find in the recipes I have chosen for this chapter, with delicious dressings to go with them

Salad Medley

PEPPER AND LAMB SALAD

This salad is best described as a 'meaty' one with the slivers of lamb making it into a substantial dish which, served with new potatoes, makes a light lunch for those hot sultry days of summer.

Serves 4.

225g (4 oz) cooked lamb
½ teaspoon paprika
1 tablespoon capers, drained
6 stalks celery, cut into chunks
1 red pepper, halved lengthwise and seeds removed
1 green pepper, halved lengthwise and seeds removed

6 tablespoons mayonnaise
1 tablespoon vinegar
Salt and pepper to taste

Cut lamb into bite size slivers or cubes. Put into a mixing bowl the celery, capers and paprika. Mix mayonnaise, vinegar and then blend with the other ingredients. Put peppers into boiling water for a few seconds, then drain and rinse under cold water. Dry peppers and then spoon into the shells the lamb mixture. Arrange in one of your prettiest salad bowls or dishes and garnish with salad leaves. Serve with baby new potatoes or crusty bread.

CRUNCHY CARROT AND NUT SALAD

This salad really is a crunchy one, with the melon giving it a moist and slightly sweet taste. I sometimes double the quantity of ingredients and make a large salad, which can be served with cold meats, cheese and fish if you are entertaining or serving a buffet lunch.

Serves 4.

1 medium Honeydew melon, de-seeded
and diced
3 medium carrots, peeled and grated
6 spring onions, sliced
75g (3 oz) raisins
1 small can of pimento
5 sticks of celery, sliced

110g (4 oz) salted peanuts
6 tablespoons French garlic dressing
1 cos lettuce
2 large hard-boiled eggs, sliced
1 small bunch watercress
Salt and pepper

Put the melon into a bowl and add the carrot, spring onions, raisins, pimento, celery and peanuts. Pour over the dressing and seasoning and toss gently. Arrange a bed of lettuce on a plate or shallow dish and spoon the salad on top. Garnish with the hard-boiled eggs and watercress.

CHICKEN AND MELON SALAD WITH MIXED HERBS

I tend to make the most of melons when they are plentiful in the shops and cheap too, so here is another recipe combining chicken and melon together with mixed herbs, giving a lovely aromatic flavour to this dish.

Serves 4.

1 Galia melon	4 generous tablespoons mayonnaise
450g (1lb) cold chopped chicken	2 tablespoons chopped mixed herbs of
1 red pepper, de-seeded and thinly sliced	your choice
1 green pepper, de-seeded and thinly sliced	Salt and pepper
Paprika	

Scoop out flesh from melon, making sure to discard pips, and put into a large salad bowl. Add chopped chicken, peppers, herbs and mayonnaise to the scooped out melon. Season and toss together until well mixed, and sprinkle with paprika.

HOT NEW POTATO MINTY SALAD

A refreshing way to serve new potatoes; the dressing can also be served over cooked meats and freshly cooked vegetables.

Serves 6.

1kg (2lb) new potatoes	2 tablespoons chopped mint
2 sprigs of mint	Salt and black pepper
1 avocado, stoned and halved	2 tablespoons French dressing (made
3 large spring onions, chopped	with cider vinegar to give it an extra bite)

Boil new potatoes in salted water with mint sprigs for about 20 minutes. While the potatoes are cooking, peel avocado and mash the halves, adding the spring onions, mint, salt and pepper. Combine into this mixture the French dressing. Drain the cooked potatoes and arrange in a serving dish, then spoon over the avocado dressing and serve immediately.

FRENCH DRESSING MADE WITH CIDER VINEGAR

This quantity of French dressing will keep for 2 or 3 weeks. Store in a cool place and use as required.

1 rounded teaspoon French mustard

1 rounded teaspoon sea salt

$\frac{1}{2}$ level teaspoon freshly-ground black pepper

300ml ($\frac{1}{2}$ pint) olive oil

Juice of 1 lemon

4 tablespoons cider vinegar

$\frac{1}{2}$ level teaspoon sugar

Put all the above ingredients into a jar with a well-fitting screw top lid and shake thoroughly.

APPLE AND CELERY SALAD

This is one of my favourite salads, and adding grapes make it just that extra bit special if you are serving it to guests.

Serves 4-6.

8 dessertspoons low fat mayonnaise

2 teaspoons paprika

4 crisp green eating apples, cored and sliced

1 celery head, thinly sliced

Salt and black pepper to taste

2 teaspoons white wine vinegar

50g (2 oz) sultanas or raisins

175g (6oz) green grapes, halved and seeded

Combine together the mayonnaise, vinegar and paprika in a large salad bowl. Add the rest of the ingredients and gently toss together.   Garnish with a few almond flakes and lettuce leaves.

PASTA AND RED PEPPER SALAD

This version of a pasta salad is very popular and moreish. It goes well with chicken and barbecued meats, and is ideal to serve for a buffet supper in the summer evenings.

Serves 6-8

450g (1lb) penne pasta quills

3 spring onions, finely chopped

50g (2 oz) toasted almond flakes

3 tablespoons parmesan cheese

1 red pepper, finely chopped

Dressing:

1 tin anchovies in oil, finely chopped

Juice of 1 lemon

1 teaspoons garlic, crushed

3 tablespoons parmesan cheese

2 tablespoons olive oil

Salt and freshly ground black pepper

1 tablespoon spiced vinegar

Cook pasta according to instructions on packet. Drain, rinse in cold water, making sure the pasta is thoroughly drained. Mix in the rest of the salad ingredients. Combine all the salad dressing ingredients and toss over the salad.

QUICK TOMATO SALAD

Choose as many good firm tomatoes as you like, according to number of guests or family, and finely slice them onto a large plate or dish. Slip slivers of garlic between the layers and then sprinkle with chopped fresh basil, salt and black pepper. Then drizzle over a generous tablespoon of olive oil and leave to infuse for several hours at room temperature, then serve.

CUCUMBER SALAD

This salad is ideal to serve as a starter, takes very little time to assemble, and makes an attractive centre piece to a dinner party table.

Serves 4.

110g (4 oz) chopped, unpeeled cucumber

1 packet lime or lemon jelly

2 tablespoons grated onion

200ml (7fl oz) boiling water

225g (8 oz) cottage cheese

50g (2 oz) flaked almonds

110g (4 oz) mayonnaise

Dissolve jelly in boiling water and add all the other ingredients, mixing them well together. Chill and serve as needed.

APPLE AND BEETROOT SALAD WITH PASTA

For some reason or other I always serve this salad at Christmas time, it goes so well with cold turkey or beef, and will keep at least 2- 3 days in the fridge too.

Serves 4.

Dressing:

450g (1lb) eating apples, diced

450g (1lb) cooked beetroot, diced

225g (8 oz) celery, chopped

225g (8 oz) pasta shapes

2 tablespoons oil

Some chopped chives

150g (5 oz) soured cream

2 tablespoons single cream

Juice of 1 lemon

2 teaspoons horseradish sauce

2 tablespoons onion, chopped

Salt and pepper to taste

Cook pasta according to instructions on packet, usually about 5 – 6 minutes. Drain and rinse well under cold water. Add oil and coat pasta. Mix all dressing ingredients and stir in apples, beetroot and celery. Keep in fridge until ready to serve. Before serving add pasta and garnish with chives.

HAM AND LEEK SALAD

This salad has a hot dressing which gives extra flavour to the ham and vegetables. If you prefer, chicken goes equally as well in this recipe.

Serves 4.

4 medium leeks, washed and sliced

1 tablespoon olive oil

1½ tablespoons dry white wine

1 dessert apple, peeled and sliced

225g (8 oz) cooked ham, sliced

50g (2 oz) spinach leaves, washed and torn up

Put the leeks in a small saucepan and add the oil. Toss the leeks until thoroughly coated in oil, cover tightly with lid and cook on a very low heat for 5 minutes. Add the wine to the pan and remove from heat. Add the remaining ingredients and toss well before turning onto serving plates. Eat immediately!

CARROT, LEEK AND ASPARAGUS SALAD

The tastes and colours in this salad make an unusually refreshing mixture, and although this recipe gives white asparagus, green will do just as well.

Serves 4.

700g (1½ lb) white or green asparagus

4 medium carrots, washed and scraped

3 medium leeks

15g (½ oz) butter

Finely grated zest and juice of 1 orange

1 tablespoon white wine vinegar

2 tablespoons olive oil

Salt and pepper

Trim asparagus and cut into equal lengths, then cook in salted boiling water for about 10 minutes and drain thoroughly. Cook carrots in salted boiling water for 7-8 minutes, drain well. Trim and slice leeks, and fry gently in melted butter for 3-4 minutes. Stir in orange zest and juice, add carrots and cook for about 2 minutes. Turn into dish and add the cooked asparagus. Whisk vinegar with oil and seasoning and drizzle over the salad. Cover and chill so that the flavours can blend, garnish with sprigs of parsley.

HOT CHICKEN AND BACON SALAD WITH PINE KERNELS

A delicious crunchy salad, which looks attractive when served in your prettiest salad bowl or in individual dishes, which is how I serve it.

Serves 4.

2 chicken breasts

6 rashers of smoked middle cut bacon

1 lollo roffo lettuce (red)

1 crisp lettuce (little gem)

Bunch watercress

50g (2 oz) pine kernels

2 tablespoons olive oil

Salt and pepper

Cut chicken and bacon into small strips. Wash lettuce and watercress and arrange in 4 individual dishes or large salad bowl. Heat one tablespoon of olive oil gently and fry chicken until cooked. Remove from heat and set aside. Then fry bacon until crispy and add chicken pieces, pine kernels and rest of oil to mixture. Spoon onto prepared lettuce while hot and serve immediately.

FRUIT SALAD CURRY

A salad with an oriental flavour and ideal to serve in the winter months when traditional salads take a back seat until spring and summer arrives.

Serves 4.

1 425g (15 oz) can diced fruit cocktail
225g (½ lb) cooking apples, peeled, cored and sliced
1 clove garlic
25g (1 oz) cornflour
300ml (½ pint) water or vegetable stock
1 tablespoon Mango chutney (or other)

1 dessertspoon tomato marmalade (or other)
Juice of ½ lemon or orange
1 tablespoon sultanas
2 tablespoons desiccated coconut soaked in 3 level tablespoons boiling water
1 teaspoon curry powder

Fry diced onion in oil on low heat, then add curry powder, garlic and cornflour. Cook for 3-4 minutes, stirring constantly. Add water or vegetable stock, juice from tin of fruit, chutney and tomato marmalade, sultanas and sliced apples. Simmer gently for 40 minutes, stirring occasionally, add coconut liquor and drained tin of fruit shortly before serving. Serve with boiled rice and hard boiled eggs.

DESSERTS AND PUDDINGS

In this chapter I've included many of the traditional puddings, as well as some of the not so traditional ones. You will also find plenty of choice when it comes to choosing a pudding or dessert that will balance your main course. I've also included some very low fat recipes, and ones that are quite easy and simple to prepare, in fact I've tried to give a tempting selection of puddings and desserts to suit every occasion and palate – I hope you will agree!

Steamed Chocolate Pudding

ORANGE AND LEMON FRUIT JELLY

This jelly is a light refreshing dessert, best served after a heavy main course. The lemons given it a nice sharp, tangy taste, and you can vary this recipe by using other fruits of your choice. Children love this dessert.

Serves 4-6.

850ml (1½ pints) of water
300ml (½ pint) lemon and orange juice
150ml (5 fl oz) sherry
225g (8 oz) caster sugar

50g (2 oz) gelatine
Rinds of 2 lemons and 2 oranges
Whites of 2 eggs
450g (1lb) orange and tangerine segments

Cut the lemon rind thinly and add to the water, lemon and orange juice, eggs whites and sugar and bring slowly to the boil. Strain the liquid and then add the gelatine which has been dissolved in a little water, whisking it in gradually. Bring back to the boil and add the sherry. Pour a little into a jelly mould and leave to set. Add a layer of orange and tangerine segments, cover with more jelly and leave to set. Gradually build up several layers in this way until all is set. Dip the mould into hot water to loosen the jelly before turning it out. Decorate with segments of orange and tangerine, and if you aren't watching calories, serve with cream.

GRAPE AND WINE JELLY

If you prefer a more sophisticated jelly, then this one will grace any dinner party table, and makes a stunning table centre for a buffet supper.

Serves 6.

300ml (½ pint) unsweetened grape juice
300ml (½ pint) dessert wine
25g (1 oz) gelatine

Small bunch of seedless green grapes
1 egg white beaten lightly
30g – 50g (1½ - 2oz) caster sugar

Combine the grape juice and wine together. Put 6 tablespoons of water into a small basin and sprinkle the gelatine over. Leave for 5 minutes. Place the basin over a pan of hot water to dissolve the gelatine. Allow to cool slightly, and add to the grape mixture. Stir to combine all ingredients. Pour into a mould and leave to set. Wash grapes and dry gently. Then take each grape and dip into the egg white, and then in the sugar. Leave to dry. Turn out the jelly when set and decorate with frosted grapes.

BLACKCURRANT QUEEN OF PUDDINGS

This is one of the great English classic puddings and a real family favourite. I have chosen a blackcurrant flavour for this recipe, but you can use any other fruit conserve you prefer.

Serves 4-6.

150g (5 oz) about 6 dessertspoons blackcurrant conserve

600ml (1 pint) skimmed milk

10g (½ oz) butter

110g (4 oz) fresh white breadcrumbs

110g (4 oz) caster sugar

Grated zest of 1 lemon

3 large eggs

Pour milk into saucepan and bring to the boil. Stir in the butter, breadcrumbs, 60g (2½ oz) sugar and lemon zest and leave for about 15-20 minutes to allow bread to swell. Separate eggs and put the whites into a large bowl and the yolks into a smaller one. Beat the yolks and whisk them into the breadcrumb mixture. Lightly butter six 5 cm (2") deep ramekins and divide the mixture between the ramekins, taking care to smooth the tops. Place on a baking tray and bake in preheated oven 180C, 350F, Gas Mark 4 for about 25-30 minutes until set. In a small saucepan melt the blackcurrant conserve over a low heat and when the puddings are cooked, remove from oven and spread the melted conserve evenly over the tops. Whisk egg whites to stiff peak, then whisk in 40g (1½ oz) sugar and spread over each ramekin, piling it in high peaks. Then sprinkle a teaspoon of sugar over the top of each pudding, place them on a baking tray and bake for a further 15 minutes until the tops are golden brown.

YOGHURT AND CHOCOLATE WHIP

This is a quick party dessert and can be made in less than 20 minutes. I must have had this recipe for years, but only recently found it tucked away in one of my old recipe books - believe me it's delicious and not too fattening if you use low-fat soft cheese.

Serves 4.

350g (12 oz) low-fat soft cheese

75g (3 oz) icing sugar

25g (1 oz) good quality cocoa powder, sieved

2 egg whites

Decoration:

2 tablespoons natural yoghurt

A little orange rind

Cream the low fat soft cheese with the sugar and cocoa until smooth. Whisk the egg whites until stiff, then fold into the soft cheese and cocoa mixture. Pipe the mixture into 4 individual dishes. Decorate with the extra yoghurt and orange rind. Place in refrigerator until required.

FRESH APRICOT MOUSSE

This dessert is pure indulgence, but I do try to make it at least once a year when the fresh apricots are around.

Serves 4-6.

450g (1lb) fresh apricots   600ml (1 pint) double cream
175g (6 oz) icing sugar

Put the apricots into a basin and cover with boiling water. Leave for a few minutes, then peel the skins off, cut in half and remove stones.   Rub the fruit through a sieve into bowl, adding the sifted icing sugar a little at a time, testing for sweetness, as you may find you like less sugar than given in the recipe. This depends on the ripeness of the apricots, which can be surprisingly sharp. Whisk cream until thick and blend with apricots. Put into a glass serving dish, and chill in refrigerator until needed.

BLACKBERRY CHEESE CAKE

The is a delicious dessert to make when blackberries are in season. Keep in refrigerator until you are ready to serve, but serve at room temperature.

Serves 6.

1 packet digestive biscuits   110g (4 oz) butter, melted
450g (1lb) blackberries (cleaned)   225g (8 oz) double cream
225g (8 oz) caster sugar   50g (2 oz) demerara sugar
225g (8 oz) low fat cream cheese   Blackberry jelly
Lemon to taste

Crush the biscuits until they make a crumb mixture. Add demerara sugar and melted butter and spread evenly over the base of an 20.5cm (8 inch) flan dish. Combine cream cheese and double cream together until smooth, add castor sugar and lemon to taste and then spread evenly over the crumb base. Place blackberries on top and glaze with blackberry jelly, which has been slightly warmed.

CRANBERRY AND SPICED APPLE PIE

This is the pie to make at Christmas time when you have some cranberries left over, or you could use apples on their own with the cinnamon giving them extra flavour.

Serves 6-8 (halve ingredients if you want to make a small pie)

Frozen shortcrust pastry
(enough to line 23cm (9 inch) pie plate
250g (9 oz) caster sugar
150g (5 oz) fresh or frozen cranberries
750g (1lb 10oz) cooking apples, peeled,
sliced and cored

2 teaspoons ground cinnamon
½ teaspoon ground nutmeg
¼ teaspoon salt
2 tablespoons apple or redcurrant jelly
melted
110g (4 oz) plain flour

In a saucepan combine 220g (7 oz) sugar with the cranberries and 1 tablespoon of water, cook gently and stir until a liquid forms, then bring to the boil, stirring constantly and the cranberries begin to burst, about 8 minutes. Then set aside to cool. On a floured surface unfold the shortcrust pastry and place on top of the pie plate, leaving some of the pastry to drop over the sides, then set aside. In a bowl combine together the apples, flour, cinnamon, nutmeg, salt and remaining sugar, and stir in the cooled cranberries. Spoon into the pastry and fold the overlapping pastry around the edges, and bake in preheated oven 230C, 450F, Gas Mark 8 for 15 minutes, then reduce heat to 180C, 350F, Gas Mark 4 until crust is golden brown and the filling is beginning to bubble (cover pastry with foil if it begins to brown too quickly). Place on wire rack to cool slightly and then spoon the melted apple jelly over the cooked pie. Sprinkle with icing sugar before serving, if desired.

APPLE AND DATE CRUMBLE

Dates and apples go well together in this recipe, giving an extra sweetness which enables you to use less sugar.

Serves 4-6.

225g (8 oz) dessert dates, stoned and halved
750g (1lb 10 oz) dessert apples, peeled
and cored
50g (2 oz) light brown sugar
½ teaspoon lemon juice

50g (2 oz) demerara sugar
25g (1 oz) porridge oats
50g (2 oz) hazelnuts, chopped
Dates to garnish

Topping:

110g (4 oz) plain flour
50g (2 oz) butter

Cut the apples into slices and put into a large pie dish together with the dates, sugar and lemon juice. **To make topping:** rub butter into flour and add sugar, oats and hazelnuts. Sprinkle this mixture evenly over the fruit and garnish with some dates. Bake in preheated oven 200C, 400F, Gas Mark 6 for about 30 minutes, or until the top is golden brown.

RHUBARB SLICES

Try to make this luscious dessert using the first young rhubarb when it first arrives in the shops, you can also use other fruit in this recipe, raspberries and gooseberries are an excellent alternative.

Makes 8-9 slices

700g (1½ lb) young rhubarb
75g (3 oz) caster sugar
Juice of 1 orange
150g (5 oz) butter

4 large eggs
75g (3 oz) desiccated coconut
110g (4 oz) plain flour
225g (8 oz) caster sugar

Wash and peel the rhubarb. Cut into slices and place in a well-buttered ovenproof dish. Sprinkle the rhubarb with the 75g (3 oz) caster sugar and the juice of 1 orange. Cover with foil and bake in preheated oven 170C, 325F, Gas Mark 3 for 20-25 minutes. Set aside to cool. Drain the juices from the cooked rhubarb into a saucepan and boil until the juices reduce to a syrup. Cream the butter and 225g (8 oz) caster sugar together, and gradually beat in 4 egg yolks singly. Beat the mixture until well combined. Whisk the remaining egg whites until stiff peaks and fold into the egg-butter mixture. Now gradually mix in the 75g (3 oz) desiccated coconut and the 110g (4 oz) plain flour. Spread this mixture onto a well-greased Swiss roll tin measuring about 30.5cm x 23cm (12" x 9"). Place the rhubarb on the mixture evenly spread in 3 rows lengthwise. Spoon over the rhubarb the reduced cooking liquid. Place in preheated oven 190C, 375F, Gas Mark 5 and bake for about 1 hour, or until golden brown. Cool, then dust with icing sugar and cut into slices. Serve with clotted cream or crème frais.

PEACH AND RICE PUDDING

This is an unusual pudding, which is really called Peach Pudding. I used to make it often when my daughter was small, she didn't like rice, as lots of small children don't, and this was one way of getting her to eat rice, albeit ground rice. I used to vary the topping and use raspberry or blackberry jelly, which made the pudding look even more attractive.

225g (8 oz) peaches (2 very large ones)
150ml (½ pint) water
Sugar to taste
2 fairly large eggs

50g (2 oz) ground rice
600ml (1 pint) semi skimmed milk
50g (2 oz) ground almonds

Poach the peaches in water for about 5 minutes. Add sugar to taste and allow to cool. Mix the ground rice to a paste with a little of the milk. Boil the rest of the milk in a saucepan and stir gradually into rice paste. Then add ground almonds, mixing well, and add sugar to taste. Add the well beaten eggs to the mixture and put into a lightly buttered fireproof dish. Bake in preheated oven 180C, 350F, Gas Mark 4 for about 30 minutes, until pudding is set. Liquidise the stewed peaches and spread over the top of the rice pudding.

APPLE AMBER

This pudding has a sharp, tangy taste, and you'll find adding a little cochineal to the apples gives them a rosy amber glow, hence it's name.

Serves 6.

900g (2lb) cooking apples
¼ teaspoon cinnamon
50g (2 oz) butter.
Juice and grated rind of 1 lemon

110g (4 oz) caster sugar
2 eggs separated
2 tablespoons caster sugar

Peel and slice apples and put into saucepan. Add cinnamon, butter, strained lemon juice and rind of lemon, and the 110g (4 oz) caster sugar. Cover and simmer until tender. Beat or liquidise the apple mixture, then stir in egg yolks. Pour into a buttered oven proof dish. Beat egg whites to a stiff peaks and stir in the 2 tablespoons of caster sugar. Then pile over the top of the apple mixture. Bake in preheated oven 140C, 275F, Gas Mark 1 until the pudding is cooked and the meringue is slightly browned, but not too much.

RASPBERRY AND ALMOND CRUMBLE

This is a change from the usual apple crumble, and using almonds in the crumble gives the topping a nice crunchy taste, gooseberries go well with the almond crumble mixture too, but you need a little more sugar to taste.

Serves 6.

2 medium punnets of raspberries
1 - 2 tablespoons sugar, or to taste
2 teaspoons cornflour
1 tablespoon lemon juice
75g (3 oz) plain flour
75g (3 oz) ground almonds

150g (5oz) butter, diced
2 teaspoons finely grated lemon rind
6 tablespoons light brown sugar
6 tablespoons flakes almonds
2 teaspoons grated orange rind

Place raspberries in a shallow, buttered baking dish, and sprinkle with sugar. Mix cornflour with lemon juice and a little water until smooth and pour over raspberries. To make topping place butter, flour, lemon rind and brown sugar in a blender and blend until mixture forms a rough crumb. Add flaked almonds and orange rind, and mix together with a fork. Sprinkle this over the raspberries and bake in preheated oven 180C, 350F, Gas Mark 4 for 30 minutes until the top is crisp and golden.

BLUEBERRY AND CRÈME FRAICHE TART

This is a dessert to serve for a special occasion, or dinner party. It's quite easy to assemble and it's best served very cold; so if you make this dessert early it can stay in the refrigerator until you are ready to serve it to your guests. To save time buy a pre-baked pastry flan from your local supermarket.

Serves 6.

300 (10½ ozs) blueberries
275g (9½ ozs) raspberries
225g (8 oz) caster sugar
6 eggs

2 teaspoons vanilla essence, optional
425 (15oz) crème fraîche
22cm (8 inch) pre-baked pastry flan

Freshen berries in a little water and pat dry, taking off any stalks. In a basin lightly beat the eggs with sugar, vanilla and crème fraîche. Then place this mixture over a saucepan of boiling water stirring continuously until the mixture is hot and starts to thicken. Place the blueberries and raspberries in the bottom of the pre-baked pie shell, then pour the cooked custard mixture over and bake in pre-heated 170C, 320F, Gas Mark 3 oven for 10-15 until the custard is set. Then chill well.

LEMON SPONGE SOUFFLÉ

This is a very old recipe I found tucked into one of my ancient cookery notebooks. It used to be very popular and I used sometimes to use an orange instead, but found I like the tangy taste of lemon better.

Serves 4.

25g (1 oz) butter	2 tablespoons of plain flour
1 teacup of caster sugar	Rind and juice of 1 lemon
2 egg yolks	1 teacup of milk

Cream the butter and sugar together and stir in the 2 egg yolks, rind and juice of 1 lemon, 2 tablespoons flour and the 1 teacup of milk. Then beat the two remaining egg whites stiffly and fold into the creamed mixture. Bake in pre-heated oven 190C, 375F, Gas Mark 5 for 35-40 minutes or until risen and golden brown.

PLUM DUFF PUDDING

This is an old favourite, which used to be tied up in a floured cloth and boiled. But for this recipe I tried steaming the pudding, which I think gave a lighter result.

Serves 6.

225g (8 oz) self-raising flour	110g (4oz), currants, raisins & sultanas
110g (4 oz) suet	75f (3 oz) caster sugar

Place all the ingredients into a fairly large bowl. Mix together with about half a teacup of milk until mixture forms into a soft, but not sticky, dough. Place the dough mixture into a suitable cloth and roll into a roly-poly shape. Tie securely, leaving room for expansion. Steam for about 3-4 hours. Turn out onto a warmed plate and sprinkle with sugar. Best served with hot custard.

Honey and Raisin Cake p95.

Baked Blackberry Bakewell Tart p92.

Double Crusted Rabbit Pie p47.

Simple Sponge Sandwich p102.

Fruity Flapjacks p107.

Buttermilk
Scones p109.

BREAD AND BUTTER PUDDING

Most of us have stale bread to use up at some time or other, and what better way than to make a bread and butter pudding. This recipe is traditional, but adding lemon and orange does give it a special taste. I sometimes grate dark chocolate between the layers of bread which gives it an even better flavour, but this is optional.

Serves 4-6

12 slices of not too stale bread	Rind of 1 lemon, grated
Butter	Rind of 1 orange grated
2 eggs	½ teaspoon vanilla extract
2 tablespoons raisins	300ml (½ pint milk)

Trim the crust from the slices of bread, and butter the slices and cut each slice in half. Place the bread slices in a well-buttered baking dish and scatter a few raisins between each layer. Warm the milk and add the vanilla essence. Separate the eggs, then whisk yolks with the vanilla flavoured milk. Whisk whites until stiff and fold into the egg and milk mixture. Pour the mixture over the bread, then sprinkle with half the grated lemon and orange rinds and bake in preheated oven 180C, 350F, Gas Mark 4 for about 40-50 minutes until pudding is set and golden brown. Use the remainder of lemon and orange rinds to decorate pudding, sprinkle with a little sugar and serve piping hot.

STEAMED CHOCOLATE PUDDING

Not long ago I wanted to make a 'no fuss' steamed chocolate pudding, but I found most of my recipes either had nuts or even fruit in the recipe, or were baked puddings, in the end I devised this pudding. The sauce is a plain chocolate one although, if you wanted to, you could add brandy or Cointreau which will give you a richer sauce.

Serves 6.

175g (6 oz) self-raising flour	150g (5 oz) caster sugar
175g (6 oz) butter	4 medium eggs
75g (3 oz) sifted cocoa	

Butter a 1½ litres (2 pint) pudding basin. Cream butter and sugar until fluffy, then add the eggs beating well each time and adding a tablespoon of flour with each egg, Then fold in remaining flour and sifted cocoa, add a little milk if mixture is too stiff. Put the mixture into basin, smooth the surface and cover with greaseproof paper and foil. Then steam for 1½ - 2 hours, testing with skewer to see pudding is cooked through.

Chocolate Sauce

175g (6 oz) good quality plain chocolate	50g (2 oz) caster sugar
50g (2 oz) butter	A little milk

Put all the ingredients into a bowl over a saucepan of simmering water. Allow all the ingredients to melt, stirring continually. If you find the sauce too thick then just add a little more milk. Pour into a jug and serve separately with chocolate pudding. And if you haven't time to make the sauce, you can be really indulgent and serve the pudding with a generous dollop of clotted cream or a rich vanilla ice cream.

BLACKBERRY BAKEWELL TART

Most fruits work well in this tart, but you can use any fruit of your choice, or whatever is in season.
Serves 6-8.

Pastry	Filling:
110g (4 oz) plain flour	110g (4 oz) butter
50g (2 oz) wholemeal flour	110g (4 oz) castor sugar
40g (1½ oz) butter	110g (4 oz) semolina
40g (1½ oz) lard	1 egg beaten
About 2 tablespoons water	1 tablespoon blackberry jelly
	110g (4 oz) blackberries

For the pastry measure flours into a bowl, then rub in fats until mixture resembles fine breadcrumbs. Bind together with water to give a stiff dough. Wrap in cling film and rest in refrigerator for about 15 minutes, then roll out on a lightly floured surface. Use to line 20cm (8 inch) flan dish, prick base and return to refrigerator. **For the filling:** Measure butter, sugar, semolina, egg into a bowl and beat well until thoroughly blended. Spread jelly over base of flan shell and arrange blackberries on top. Spoon the semolina mixture over the blackberries, spread evenly and bake in preheated oven 200C, 400F, Gas Mark 6 for about 35 minutes until golden brown and pastry is cooked. Serve hot or cold.

SPICY BREAD PUDDING

This pudding is ideal for using up those crusts of bread we find lurking at the back of our bread bins. You can use any fruit you may have in your store cupboard, and I find a tablespoon of marmalade enhances the flavour of this simple pudding, which is so easy to assemble and make.

Serves 6.

225g (8 oz) stale bread	50g (2 oz) mixed peel
110g (4 oz) sultanas	50g (2 oz) suet
50g (2 oz) brown sugar	½ teaspoon mixed spice
1 egg	A little milk
1 tablespoon orange marmalade (preferably homemade)	

Break the bread into small pieces and soak in cold water for at least 1/2 hour; then strain and squeeze dry as possible. Put into a basin and beat out the lumps with a fork. Add the dried fruit, sugar, suet, peel and mixed spice and marmalade and mix well. Add beaten egg and enough milk to enable the mixture to drop easily from the spoon. Put into a greased baking tin and bake in preheated oven 170C, 325F, Gas Mark 3 for about 1 hour. When cooked dredge with sugar and serve with custard.

CAKES AND PASTRIES

Today a majority of cakes and pastries can also be used as desserts, but in this chapter I've endeavoured to write about cakes and pastries that go well with an afternoon cup of tea. However, that doesn't stop the cook serving them as a dessert if she wishes, so it's really all a matter of choice. There are old favourites such as Apple Cake, to the more elaborate Blackberry Milles Feuilles.

Simple Sponge Sandwich

HONEY AND RAISIN CAKE

This is a substantial cake ideal to take on picnics or put into a lunch-box.

150g (5 oz) butter or margarine

150g (5 oz) soft brown sugar

2 eggs

2 tablespoons runny honey

225g (8 oz) wholemeal flour

1 teaspoon baking powder

1 teaspoon mixed spice

110g (4 oz) seeded raisins

150ml (¼ pint) milk

Cream butter or margarine, then beat in the two eggs separately and add the honey. Sieve flour, baking powder and spice. Fold in flour mixture into the creamed mixture, adding the raisins and finally the milk. Grease and line a 18cm (7 inch) cake tin and put mixture into tin, and bake in preheated oven 180C, 350F, Gas Mark 4 for 1½ hours until cooked through and golden brown.

CHOCOLATE AND APPLE SAUCE CAKE

This is one of my favourite variations on the traditional Apple Cake with the two flavours of apple and chocolate blending well together.

300ml (½ pint) unsweetened apple sauce

110g (4 oz) butter

2 eggs

175g (6 oz) caster sugar

115g (8 oz) self-raising flour

¼ teaspoon baking powder

½ teaspoon allspice

110g (4 oz) sultanas

2 dessertspoons cocoa

½ teaspoon bicarbonate of soda

1 teaspoon cinnamon

¼ teaspoon salt

Liquidise or beat well together the first four ingredients. Sieve together all the dry ingredients and add sultanas. Add the apple sauce mixture and combine together. Pour batter into a greased 20.5 cm (8 inch) cake tin and bake in preheated oven 150C, 300F, Gas Mark 2 for about 1½ hours. Test with skewer to make sure cake is cooked through.

CHOCOLATE BANANA LOAF

This cake came from the Friends of Boxford School Cook Book, and is almost an all in one mix which doesn't take long to prepare. The texture is lovely and moist and the taste is delicious.

Makes 12-14 slices

150g (5½ oz) butter at room temperature
150g (5½ oz) good quality plain chocolate
150g (5½ oz) light muscovada sugar
3 medium bananas, weighing about
3½ ozs each, mashed
3 eggs beaten
200g (7 oz) plain flour

Icing:

100g (3½ oz) good quality plain chocolate, broken into pieces
25g (1 oz) butter
50g (2 oz) icing sugar
1 tablespoon milk
2 teaspoons baking powder

Preheat oven 150C, 300F, Gas Mark 2. Grease a 900g (2lb) loaf tin and line with grease-proof paper. In a medium non-stick pan (this is the beauty of this recipe, there is only a pan to wash up!), gently heat the butter, sugar and chocolate until melted. Stir well and remove from the heat. Add the bananas and eggs, then sift in the flour and baking powder. Mix to a smooth, thick batter. Pour the mixture into the prepared tin and bake for 1 hour until the cake has risen and feels firm in the centre when lightly pressed with your fingertips. Remove from the oven and cool in the tin for 5 minutes. Turn out onto a wire rack to cool completely. **To make the icing:** In a small non-stick pan, melt the chocolate with the butter. Sift the icing sugar, then stir in the milk and beat well. Spread over the top of the cake. Allow to set before cutting into thick slices.

MARMALADE BUN LOAF

This bun loaf is delicious sliced and buttered, and is best kept for a day before slicing and eating, if you can!

8 tablespoons sifted self-raising flour
2 tablespoons golden syrup
1 tablespoon black treacle
1½ tablespoons good quality marmalade

2 tablespoons milk
2 tablespoons water
2 tablespoons sultanas
1 tablespoons mixed peel

Combine all the dry ingredients together. Make a well in the centre and add treacle, golden syrup and marmalade. Add milk and water gradually and stir well all together and beat thoroughly. Turn into a 450g (1lb) loaf tin and bake in preheated oven 325C, 170C, Gas Mark 3 for at least 45-50 minutes. Cool on rack and when cold wrap tightly in foil.

GINGERBREAD CAKE

I love any form of gingerbread and this cake is really delicious with the raisins adding a nice fruity taste.

225g (8 oz) soft dark sugar
110g (4 oz) butter
1 small teacup of milk
225g (8 oz) black treacle
3 eggs

225g (8 oz) plain flour
1 level teaspoon bicarbonate of soda
2 level teaspoons ground ginger
75g (3 oz) raisins

Melt the sugar, treacle and butter in a saucepan and when cool add the milk. Add a little of the sifted flour, bicarbonate of soda and ginger followed by a little of the beaten egg. Repeat this process until the ingredients are used. Lastly, fold in the raisins. Bake in preheated oven 170C, 325F, Gas Mark 3 for 1¼ hours, or until cooked through.

MINCEMEAT CAKE

When I make my mincemeat ready for Christmas mince pies, I usually make extra pots to have by me and to give away. This cake is a rich and fairly dark fruit cake, which can be stored for up to one month and marzipanned and iced if you wish – I usually just leave mine plain and freeze it until required.

225g (8 oz) butter
175g (6 oz) soft dark brown sugar
3 eggs

350g (12 oz) plain flour
1 level teaspoon baking powder
700g (1½ lb) mincemeat

Beat the butter until soft. Add sugar and beat mixture again until light and fluffy Beat the eggs adding to the mixture gradually and beating well. Sift the flour with baking powder, and then lightly fold into mixture with the mincemeat. Grease and line a 23cm (9 inch) cake tin and turn the mixture into the tin, leaving the centre slightly hollow. Then bake in preheated oven 180C, 350F, Gas Mark 4 for about 1½ - 2 hours. Test with a skewer to see if cake is cooked through. Cool in tin for about 25 minutes then turn out on wire tray to cool completely. The cake can now be stored for up to one month wrapped in cling film and foil, or you can put into the freezer and store for up to 6 months.

RHUBARB CAKE

A delicious moist cake, which can be enjoyed either at teatime or as a dessert served with cream or custard.

150g (5oz) soft margarine	**For the topping:**
225g (8 oz) self-raising flour	450g (1lb) rhubarb
2 eggs	175g (6 oz) granulated sugar
Grated rind and juice of 1 medium orange	1 level teaspoon ground cinnamon
2 tablespoons milk	1 level tablespoons self-raising flour

Put the margarine, sugar, sifted flour, eggs, orange rind and juice and the milk into a mixing bowl. Stir the ingredients together and when they are thoroughly combined, beat the mixture well for at least two minutes until it is light and fluffy. Lightly grease an 20.5cm (8 inch) spring clip cake tin and turn the mixture into the tin. **For the topping:** Trim and wash the rhubarb and cut into 1 cm (½ inch) pieces. Scatter the pieces over the top of the cake. Mix the sugar with the cinnamon and flour and sprinkle the mixture over the rhubarb. Bake in preheated oven 190C, 375F, Gas Mark 5 for 1½ hours, or until cooked through. Loosen cake from the sides of the tin immediately the cake is cooked and cool it in the tin for 10 minutes before transferring it to a wire tray to cool completely.

BLACKBERRY MILLES FEUILLES

This version of milles feuilles is quite easy and I much prefer it to the round 'mille' as you can cut into slices and serve.

Makes 6 slices.

350g (12 oz) packet frozen puff pastry	150ml (¼ pint) double cream
300g (10½ oz) blackberries	150ml (¼ pint) single cream
Sugar to taste	

Divide pastry into three and roll out each piece (thinly) into a strip about 10cm (4 inches) wide and as long as possible. Place on a slightly damp baking sheet and bake in preheated oven 230C, 450F, Gas Mark 8 (about 12 minutes) until brown and well risen. Remove from oven and allow to cool. Mash the blackberries with sugar. Whip the double cream, add the single cream and whip again. Trim edges of pastry when cooled, and spread first strip of pastry with mashed fruit, cover with cream and place another piece of pastry on top. Spread again with mashed blackberries and cream and cover with third piece, the smooth side uppermost. Press lightly, but firmly together. **To ice top of 'mille':** Put 225g (8 oz) icing sugar into a saucepan with enough water to mix to a cream, warm slightly and coat over the top of the pastry. Cut into slices to serve.

ORANGE CAKE

This is a light cake, delicately flavoured with orange, and as it hasn't any icing it will freeze for up to one month – any longer and it will lose its flavour.

110g (4 oz) plain flour
50g (2 oz) cornflour
4 eggs
200g (7 oz) butter, melted

Vanilla essence
Rind and pulp of 1 orange finely chopped
200g (7 oz) caster sugar

Beat the eggs with the sugar until thick. Sieve the plain flour. Gently fold this into the beaten eggs, add the cornflour, but do not beat again after adding the cornflour. Stir in the warmed butter. Add the vanilla essence to taste and finally the orange. Grease and line a 20.5cm (8 inch) cake tin. Pour mixture into tin and bake in preheated oven190C, 375F, Gas Mark 5 for about 45-50 minutes, until firm to touch and golden brown. Turn out to cool on a wire rack and, when quite cold, dust with sifted icing sugar.

CARROT AND COCONUT CAKE

A carrot cake with a difference, in that the coconut gives it a special flavour from the traditional carrot cake, which usually has a cream cheese topping, and is therefore more rich and not so kind to the waistline!

Serves 6-8.

175g (6 oz) caster sugar
2 rounded tablespoons runny honey
280g (10 oz) carrots, scraped & grated
110g (4 oz) unsweetened coconut
110g (4 oz) walnuts, chopped

175g (6 oz) self-raising wholemeal flour
240ml (8fl oz) sunflower oil
3 large eggs
1 teaspoon cardamom
$\frac{1}{2}$ teaspoon salt

Put the caster sugar and the honey into a large mixing bowl. Add the sunflower oil and whisk until well mixed. Whisk in the eggs, one at a time until all combined, and continue whisking until the mixture is light and frothy. Mix the spice and salt into the flour and then whisk the flour into the egg mixture a little at a time until thoroughly mixed. Stir in the grated carrots, coconut and the chopped walnuts and pour the mixture into a greased and lined 20.5 (8 inch) round cake tin. Bake in preheated oven 180C, 350F, Gas Mark 4 for $1\frac{1}{2}$ - $1\frac{3}{4}$ hours. Test with a skewer in the centre of the cake to see the cake is cooked through.

FRUITY TEA LOAF

This is a good standby cake when you want to make something quick and easy for tea. To bring out the full flavour of this loaf I find it's best to keep it wrapped in foil for at least 24 hours.

225g (8oz) self-raising flour

150ml (¼ pint) cold strained tea

110g (4 oz) soft brown sugar

225g (8 oz) mixed dried fruit & peel

1 medium egg

Pinch of salt

Combine dried fruit and sugar together in mixing bowl and pour tea over mixture. Add sieved flour, salt and lightly beaten egg. When all the ingredients are well mixed together, pour mixture into a greased and lined 450g (1lb) loaf tin and bake in preheated oven 190C, 375F, Gas Mark 5 for about an hour, or until cooked through.

RASPBERRY AND CREAM SWISS ROLL

I think Swiss rolls are best eaten on the day they are made. You will find this recipe makes an irresistible light airy cake, which is a special teatime treat.

75g (3 oz) plain flour

Filling:

3 eggs, size 2

3 tablespoons raspberry jam

75g (3 oz) caster sugar

200g (7 oz) double cream

1 tablespoon hot water

Pinch of salt.

Sift flour and salt into a large mixing bowl. Place the eggs and the sugar in a large mixing bowl over a saucepan of hot water. Whisk them very hard until pale and thick enough to leave a trail when you lift the whisk. Remove bowl from the heat and quickly fold in about half the flour, using a metal spoon. Repeat with remaining flour and fold in the hot water, mixing evenly and gently. Grease and line a Swiss roll tin 30 x 20cm (12" x 8"). Slit corners to overlap for neat shape. Pour mixture into the prepared tin, tilting it so that it spreads evenly into the corners. Bake in preheated oven 220C, 425F, Gas Mark 7 for about 10-12 minutes, until well risen and springy to the touch. Have ready a sheet of greaseproof paper which has been sprinkled with caster sugar. Quickly turn out the cake onto the paper and carefully peel off the lining paper. Using a sharp knife, trim off the crisp edges of the cake. Roll up from one short edge, with the greaseproof paper inside, and allow Swiss roll to cool. Whip cream until it hold its shape. Carefully unroll the cooled Swiss roll and spread with the raspberry jam, then spread the cream on top of the jam and gently roll up the Swiss Roll. Sprinkle with icing sugar and serve immediately.

JAM TARTS

There's nothing to beat real homemade jam tarts, although I have to confess that I don't make them as often as I used to. The secret in making a good jam tart is to roll the pastry as thinly as possible, and not to overfill the pastry cases with jam. In this recipe I have given ingredients for pastry, but today you can buy as good as you can make shortcrust pastry from shops – and it does save time!

110g (4 oz) plain flour	A little milk
1 tablespoon caster sugar	Pinch of salt
50g (2 oz) butter	Jam of your choice

Sieve the flour, salt and sugar into a large mixing bowl. Rub in the butter until the mixture resembles fine crumbs. Add just enough milk to mix to a dough. Knead until smooth and then leave for 2 hours in a cool place to rest. Roll the pastry as thinly as possible and cut into rounds with floured cutter, making sure the rounds are one size larger than the patty tins you are using. Line the pans with dough, pressing evenly into the side. Add your jam and bake in preheated oven 200C, 400F, Gas Mark 6 for about 12 – 15 minutes.

BANANA APPLE MUFFINS

This is another recipe from the Friends of Boxford School Cookbook. Children love these muffins, and the combined flavours of banana and apple is delicious.

50g (2 oz) wholemeal flour	1 large ripe mashed banana
50g (2 oz) wholemeal self-raising flour	½ coarsely grated green apple
175g (6 oz) caster sugar	120ml (4fl oz) oil
¼ teaspoon ground nutmeg	180ml (6 fl oz) milk

Brush melted butter into 12 muffin cups. Place flours, sugar and nutmeg into a large mixing bowl. Make a well in the centre and add the fruit. Combine eggs, oil and milk in a bowl or jug. Pour all at once into dry ingredients. Using a wooden spoon stir for 1 minute or until ingredients are just combined. Spoon mixture into prepared muffin tins, filling two-thirds full. Bake in preheated oven 180C, 350F, Gas Mark 4 for 25 minutes, or until puffed and lightly golden. Turn onto wire tray to cool.

SOMERSET CREAM CAKE

A very old recipe which was given to me by a friend when I lived in Somerset. Surprisingly it doesn't have cream in the recipe, but the cake does have a creamy taste when baked. I sometimes split it and fill with a butter cream or lemon curd if it's for a special occasion.

110g (4 oz) butter

110g (4 oz caster sugar

110g (4oz) self-raising flour

Vanilla essence

50g (2oz) corn flour

$\frac{1}{2}$ teaspoon baking powder

2 eggs

Cream fat and sugar together. Add beaten eggs and vanilla essence. Then lightly fold in flour and baking powder.   Bake in preheated oven 190C, 375F, Gas Mark 5 for an hour, or until cake is cooked through. **To make butter cream filling:** Beat 75g (3oz) unsalted butter and 150g (5oz) icing sugar to a cream. Then add a few drops of vanilla essence, spread between cake and dust with icing sugar.

SIMPLE SPONGE SANDWICH

This must be one of the simplest of sponges to make. It always turns out well when I make it and although it's a very old recipe which uses margarine, I use butter which works just as well and, I think, makes it lighter.

2 eggs

75g (3 oz) butter

110g (4 oz) caster sugar

110g (4 oz) self-raising flour

1 teaspoon baking powder

25g (1 oz) corn flour

Cream butter and sugar in mixing bowl. Beat eggs well, then add sieved flour, corn flour and baking powder and eggs alternately to butter and sugar mixture. Put into a large prepared sandwich tin and bake in preheated oven 190C, 375F, Gas Mark 5 for about 20 minutes. When cold, cut and spread with jam or whipped cream.

CHOCOLATE LAYER CAKE

This is an ideal cake to make for a special occasion, with an orange flavoured topping to give it a tangy taste.

1½ level tablespoons cocoa, sieved

3 tablespoons boiling water

175g (6 oz) Stork soft margarine

175g (6 oz) caster sugar

3 eggs

175g (6 oz) self raising-flour, sieved

Filling and Topping:

Stork margarine icing (orange flavoured)

120g (4½ oz) Stork margarine

350g (12 oz) icing sugar, sieved

3 teaspoons boiling water.

Blend cocoa with water. Cool. Cream Stork and sugar together, then beat in cocoa mixture. Beat in eggs, one at a time, adding a little sieved flour each time. Divide equally between three 18cm (7 inch) tins, or two 20.5cm (8 inch) sandwich tins lined in bottoms with greaseproof paper Bake in preheated oven 180C, 350F, Gas Mark 4 for 25-30 minutes for 19cm (7 inch) size or 35-40 minutes for 20.5cm (8 inch) size. Turn out, remove papers and cool on wire trays. **To make orange flavoured icing:** Cream stork and half sieved icing sugar together until very light. Beat in remaining icing sugar with squash, until again very light. Sandwich three 18cm (7 inch) cakes or two 20.5cms (8 inch) cakes together with icing.

BISCUITS, SCONES, ROLLS AND BREADS

It's always nice to have some homemade biscuits to go with a cup of coffee or tea when friends call, and in this chapter you will find sweet and savoury scones as well as breads and rolls to eat for breakfast or at tea time. When making scones it's always a good idea to bake a double batch so that you can freeze them for a later date.

Breads and Rolls

CHOCOLATE MACAROONS

Macaroons are quite easy to make, and these make a nice change from the traditional ones as they are flavoured with chocolate.

110g (4 oz) ground almonds

25g (1 oz) butter or margarine, melted

110g (4 oz) caster sugar

60g (2½ ozs) drinking chocolate

2 egg whites

Blanched almonds

Grease or line a baking sheet with rice paper. Whip the egg whites until stiff, then fold in the dry ingredients and melted butter or margarine. Place in small heaps on baking sheet, putting a blanched almond on top of each macaroon. Bake in preheated oven 170C, 325F, Gas Mark 3 until firm and cooked through, about 25 minutes.

GINGER BISCUITS

A firm crisp biscuit with the strong full flavour of ginger, and keeps well if stored in a good airtight tin.

225g (8 oz) plain flour

75g (3 oz) butter

110g (4 oz) caster sugar

Pinch of bicarbonate of soda

1 dessertspoon ground ginger

1 dessertspoon black treacle

Half medium egg

Beat the softened butter and sugar to a cream and add the beaten egg. Then add the dry ingredients, adding the treacle half-way. Knead the mixture into a dough and roll out as thinly as possible on a floured board and cut into rounds with a plain large cutter. Bake in preheated oven 180C, 350F, Gas Mark 4 for about 10-15 minutes until brown and crisp.

OATMEAL BISCUITS

These biscuits are nice eaten buttered with cheese for supper, or spread with honey for breakfast.

1104g (4 oz) plain flour

25g (1 oz) caster sugar

50g (2 oz) butter

1 egg

50g (2 oz) fine oatmeal

Mix all the dry ingredients together, then add the melted butter and the beaten egg, adding a little milk if the mixture is too dry. Roll out on a lightly floured surface and cut into rounds with cutter. Bake on a greased and floured baking tin in preheated oven 180C, 350F, Gas Mark 4, about 15-20 minutes, until a pale golden brown.

LEMON WHOLEMEAL BISCUITS

I sometimes add currants to these biscuits, but this is optional as they taste just as good without.

110g (4 oz) butter or margarine

175g (6 oz) self-raising wholemeal flour

110g (4 oz) brown moist sugar

75g (3 oz) currants (optional)

1 large lemon, or two small ones

35g ($1\frac{1}{2}$ oz) bran

1 medium egg

Pinch of salt

Cream butter or margarine with sugar and finely grated lemon peel. Mix in the beaten egg with flour and salt and add currants. Roll teaspoons of mixture in bran to form a ball and place on a greased baking tray. Flatten to half depth of the biscuit with a fork. Bake in preheated oven 190C, 375F, Gas Mark 5. for 15 – 20 minutes, until golden brown.

CHEESY SHORTBREAD BISCUITS

These are ideal to serve to your guests with pre-supper drinks or dinner.

110g (4 oz) butter, softened

$\frac{1}{2}$ teaspoon dry mustard

50g (2 oz) semolina

110g (4 oz) grated mature Cheddar cheese

85g ($3\frac{1}{2}$ oz) self-raising flour

Put all the ingredients into a food mixer and whiz altogether. Take mixture out of mixer and roll into small balls. Put onto a greased baking sheets and flatten with a fork. Bake in preheated oven 180C, 350F, Gas Mark 4 for 15 – 20 minutes.

BUTTER AND CHERRY BISCUITS

These biscuits are really another version of shortbread and the mixture will yield at least 18 biscuits.

175g (6 oz) butter

50g (2 oz) icing sugar

½ teaspoon vanilla essence

175g (6 oz) plain flour

Glacé cherries to decorate

Cream butter, sugar and vanilla essence. Stir in the flour and put all the mixture into a forcing bag. Then pipe 18 whirls and decorate with a cherry on top of each whirl. Bake in preheated oven 170C, 320F, Gas Mark 3 for about 20 minutes. Allow to cool for 5 minutes and then lift off tray to cool completely on a wire tray.

FRUITY FLAPJACKS

This recipe breaks away from the traditional flapjack which is usually crisp and nutty. If you don't want to use mincemeat try using the same quantity of mixed dried fruit which will give the flapjack a closer texture.

450g (1lb) porridge oats

50g (2 oz) wholemeal flour

200g (7 oz) margarine

225g (8 oz) mincemeat, or dried fruit

Grated rind of an orange

50g (2 oz) golden syrup

110g (4 oz) Demerara sugar

Melt the margarine with the syrup and sugar. Add the mincemeat or dried fruit and orange rind. Mix together the oats and flour and stir into the mixture. Spoon the mixture into a greased baking tin and flatten with the back of a wooden spoon. Mark into squares or fingers and bake in preheated oven 180C, 350F, Gas Mark 4 for 25-30 minutes until golden brown. Leave to cool for a few minutes and cut into squares or fingers while still warm. When completely cold, store in an airtight tin.

FRUIT SCONES

This recipe makes really light scones.   It's always best to eat scones the day they are made or freeze them.

175g (6 oz) self-raising flour
1 level teaspoon baking powder
25g (1 oz) lard
25g (1 oz) margarine

25g (1 oz) caster sugar
150ml (5fl oz) milk
40g (1½ oz) mixed dried fruit

Sieve flour and baking powder into a mixing bowl, and then rub the fats into the flour. Stir in the sugar and dried fruit and stir in the milk to make a soft dough. Roll out lightly on a floured surface, about 2cm (¾ inch) thick and cut out with a plain 5cm (2 inch) cutter and put onto a greased baking sheet. Dust with extra flour or brush with a little milk and bake in preheated oven 200C, 400F, Gas Mark 6 for 10-12 minutes until risen and golden.

HERB AND CHEESE SCONES

I found this recipe from a newspaper cutting in one of my old cookery books. I've adapted it a little by using Cheddar cheese instead of Gruyere and it usually makes 14-16 scones.

150g (5 oz) butter, cut into small pieces
450g (1lb) plain flour
25g (1 oz) baking powder
300ml (10 fl oz) warm milk

1 tablespoon chopped fresh herbs
(parsley, chives, tarragon & dill)
110g (4 oz) Cheddar cheese

Mix the pieces of butter into the flour and baking powder until it is the texture of ground almonds. Mix in the chopped herbs and grated Cheddar cheese with the milk which has been heated gently. Gently knead the dough and then let it rest for an hour. Roll out onto a floured surface to a 2cm (¾ inch) thickness and cut out with 5cm (2 inch) cutter. Place on a greased baking sheet and let the scones rest for a further ten minutes. Brush with beaten egg and bake in preheated oven 190C, 375F, Gas Mark 5 for about 20-25 minutes.

CHEESE SCONES

I've included another scone recipe with just cheese added, as I find many friends ask me for this particular recipe and its very popular on the village bazaar stalls.

225g (8 oz) plain flour

¼ teaspoon salt

½ teaspoon dry mustard

Pinch of cayenne pepper

2 teaspoons cream of tartar

35g (1½ oz) butter

75g (3 oz) grated Cheddar cheese

150ml (5fl oz) milk

Sieve together all the dry ingredients, rub in butter until mixture resembles fine breadcrumbs. Add grated cheese and bind together with milk to form a soft dough. Turn onto a lightly floured working surface and roll out to a 1cm (½ inch) thickness and cut into round with a 5cm (2 inch) plain cutter. Put scones on a baking tray and bake for 10 minutes in preheated oven 230C, 450F, Mark 8 for about 10 minutes.

BUTTERMILK SCONES

This recipe makes ten light airy scones and are best served for tea spread with butter and your favourite jam!

225g (8 oz) self-raising flour

50g (2 oz) butter or margarine

150ml (5fl oz) buttermilk

½ teaspoon salt

Combine flour and salt together in a mixing bowl, and rub in the butter or margarine until the mixture resembles breadcrumbs. Make a well in the centre and gradually stir in the buttermilk. Knead the dough until it is soft and has no cracks in it. Lightly roll out the dough on a floured surface to a thickness of 1cm (½ inch). Cut into rounds with 5cm (2 inch) scone cutter. Place scones on a greased and floured baking tray and bake in preheated oven 200C, 400F, Gas Mark 6.

MILK ROLLS

These rolls can be made in next to no time and ready for breakfast as they don't need extra time to rise.

225g (8 oz) plain flour ½ teaspoon salt
¼ teaspoon baking powder 50g (2 oz) butter or margarine
½ teaspoon cream of tartar Milk to mix with little sugar

Sieve the flour, baking powder and cream of tartar and salt together in a mixing bowl. Rub in the butter or margarine, and then mix to a soft dough with the sweet milk. Roll out to about 5mm (¼ inch) thick and cut into squares. Fold each square over into two, sprinkle a little flour over each roll and bake in a hot oven 230C, 450F, Gas Mark 8 for 15 minutes.

SPICY APPLE MUFFINS

50g (2 oz) butter 1 teaspoon baking powder
50g (2 oz) caster sugar 75g (3 oz) chopped eating apple
1 egg 1 tablespoon milk
110g (4 oz) white self raising flour ¼ teaspoon cinnamon

Cream the butter and sugar together, and then beat in the egg. Add sieved flour with the nutmeg, cinnamon and baking powder. Mix thoroughly and add the chopped apple and milk. When all well combined put into 12 paper muffin cases in a bun tin and bake in preheated oven 200C, 400F, Gas mark 6 for 10-15 minutes until risen and cooked through.

HOT CROSS BUNS

Hot cross buns are delicious eaten straight out of the oven or lightly toasted for breakfast or afternoon tea. Try to make an extra amount and freeze them.

450g (1lb) granary flour 50g (2 oz) butter
1 teaspoon salt 1 sachet of Easy Blend Yeast
1 teaspoon mixed spice 110g (4 oz) dried fruit
½ teaspoon nutmeg 1 beaten egg
50g (2 oz) brown sugar

Combine the flour, salt, spices and sugar together in a large mixing bowl. Rub in the butter. Stir in the yeast, fruit and 300ml (10fl oz) hand hot water. Knead the dough until firm and well mixed. Cover and leave to rise in a warm place until doubled. Turn dough onto a floured working surface and knead again. Divide into 15 or 16 buns and place on baking trays and leave to rise. Brush buns with beaten egg and, if you have some left over pastry strips, roll out and cut into crosses to put on top of the buns. Bake in preheated oven 200C, 400F, Gas Mark 6.

LARDY CAKE

This is another very old recipe and made often in the village in Somerset where I grew up. Traditionally lard or dripping was used, when people kept a pig and used the lard which came from the flead, which is a thin inner membrane of the pig. Nowadays we can buy this special West Country teatime loaf, usually made with yeast, but in this recipe I've substituted butter or margarine.

450g (1lb) plain white flour	3-4 tablespoons milk
225g (8 oz) butter or margarine	1 teaspoon baking powder
225g (8 oz) soft brown sugar	2 teaspoons mixed spice
225g (8 oz) – 300g (10½ oz) mixed dried fruit	A little granulated sugar
4 eggs	

Sift flour, baking powder and spice into a large mixing bowl. Rub in butter or margarine and then add the sugar and fruit. Add the milk and the beaten eggs and mix to a dropping consistency. Grease and line a 23cm (9 inch) or 25.5cm (10 inch) cake tin, or a loaf tin, and scatter the surface with the granulated sugar. Bake in preheated oven 180C, 350F, Gas Mark 4 for about 1½ hours until nice and firm and golden brown.

FINE TEXTURED BROWN LOAF

An easy to mix loaf which goes well with a bowl of soup on a cold winter's day.

375g (12 oz) plain wholemeal flour	1 teaspoon cream of tartar
110g (4 oz) plain white flour	1 teaspoon golden syrup
1 teaspoon salt	Buttermilk or sour milk to mix
1 small teaspoon baking powder	35g (1½ oz) margarine

Sieve baking powder, salt and cream of tartar into a large mixing bowl. Add wholemeal and white flour. Rub in margarine and add syrup. Then mix to a soft dough with the milk. Turn onto a floured surface, sprinkle with wholemeal flour and pat into a round flat cake. Cut into farls and bake in a preheated oven 230C, 450F, Gas Mark 8 for 25-30 minutes.

WHOLEWHEAT TEA BREAD

This is a real standby loaf, which is ideal for picnics or served sliced and spread with butter for tea.

225g (8 oz) self-raising whole-wheat flour
120ml (4fl oz) milk
½ teaspoon mixed spice
2 eggs
75g (3 oz) butter

110g (4 oz) light brown sugar
25g (1 oz) sultanas
25g (1 oz) prunes, pitted & chopped
25g (1 oz) ready to eat dried apricots
Pinch of salt

Sift the flour, salt and mixed spice into a large mixing bowl. Stir in the sugar, then rub in the butter until the mixture resembles fine breadcrumbs. Beat the eggs and milk together and add to the mixture with all the dried fruit, stirring well to mix thoroughly. Turn the mixture into a greased and lined 1kg (2lb) loaf tin and bake in preheated oven 170C, 325F, Gas Mark 3 for just over an hour, or until well risen and golden brown. Cool tea bread in tin for about 10 minutes and then transfer to wire tray to cool completely.

ONION AND OLIVE BREAD

An easy bread to make, which goes well in the summer with a salad or soup on a cold winter's day.

350g (12 oz) self-raising flour
25g (1 oz) butter
1 medium onion, peeled and chopped
175ml (6fl oz) milk

1 tablespoon mixed fresh herbs
3 eggs
110g (4 oz) pitted black olives
Salt and black pepper

Melt butter in pan and cook the chopped onion with the mixed herbs over a low heat for about 10 minutes, until softened. Set aside and leave to cool. When cooled mix in the beaten eggs. Sift flour, salt and pepper into a bowl and mix in the onion and herbs. Add the milk and mix well, but do not beat. Stir in the olives and pour the mixture into greased and lined 18cm (7 inch) loose bottomed round cake tin or a loaf tin. Bake in pre-heated oven 200C, 400F, Gas Mark 6 for about 1-1½ hours until risen and golden brown.

BASIC WHITE BREAD

Makes 1 x 900g (2lb) or 2 x 450g (1lb) loaves

700g (1½lb) strong plain flour

1 tsp salt

15g (½oz) lard

1 sachet Easy Blend dried yeast (or 20g (¾oz) fresh yeast)

425ml 15floz) hand hot water

Beaten egg or milk to glaze

Sift the flour and salt into a bowl. Rub in lard. Stir in the dried yeast then add the water. (if using fresh yeast, dissolve in a little hand hot water, then add to the flour with the remaining liquid). Mix ingredients together to form a dough. Turn the mixture onto a floured surface and knead together for 5 minutes or until smooth and elastic. Place the dough in a lightly oiled plastic bag and leave in a warm place until doubled in size. Turn the dough onto a floured surface and knead again. Leave whole if making 1 loaf or cut in half if making 2 smaller loaves. Shape and place in greased loaf tins. Cover and leave to prove in a warm place until well risen. Glaze bread with beaten egg or milk and bake in preheated oven 240C, 475F, Gas Mark 9, until loaf is risen, well-browned and shrinking slightly from sides of the tin. Loaf should sound hollow when tapped on the bottom.

JELLIES, JAMS, CHUTNEYS AND RELISHES

In this chapter there are many homemade flavours to enjoy and relish. Although the making of homemade preserves, chutneys and relishes does take time and effort, its all worthwhile as they are far more tasty than those produced commercially and are a lot more economical.

Seville Marmalade

MINT AND APPLE JELLY

This jelly has a tangy minty flavour, which goes well with cold and roast pork. I find its best to make it in very small quantities, as you can get the ingredients all the year round.

1.4kg (3 lb) cooking apples
4-5 stalks of fresh mint
300ml (10fl oz) water

300ml (10fl oz) white wine vinegar
5 tablespoons mint, finely chopped
Sugar

Roughly quarter the apples without peeling or coring and with the stalks of mint simmer in water until the apples are soft. Add vinegar and boil for 5 minutes. Strain through jelly bag. To every pint of strained juice add 450g (1lb) of sugar. Bring to the boil and simmer until all the sugar has dissolved, stirring continuously. Then boil rapidly until the mixture sets when tested on a plate. Add chopped mint and boil for a further 2 minutes. Pour into warmed pots and seal in the usual way. Makes 2 - 450g (1lb) pots.

MUSCAT JELLY

This recipe makes a delicious red jelly with a muscatel flavour – tip – don't squeeze your jelly bag or muslin to hasten juice extraction or you will risk a cloudy jelly!

Quantity of gooseberries (depending how much jelly you want to make)
Sugar
Water

12 heads of elderflowers

Cover gooseberries with water and simmer for 2 hours. Strain as for jelly. To each pint of liquid add 450g (1lb) sugar. Stir until sugar is dissolved and then boil for 10 minutes. Three minutes before the jelly is ready, add the 12 heads of elderflowers tied in muslin. Pour into warmed jars and seal.

RASPBERRY AND REDCURRANT JELLY

I sometimes use strawberries instead of redcurrants in this recipe, and find it makes a beautifully flavoured jelly, you just need to add juice from half a lemon to make it set.

900g (2lb) raspberries
900g (2lb) redcurrant

Water

Pick over fruit and clean, then put fruit into preserving pan and add water. Simmer gently until the fruit is very soft. Strain through a jelly bag and measure the juice, allowing 450g (1lb) sugar to each 600ml (1 pint) of juice. Heat the juice gently, stirring the sugar until dissolved. Boil rapidly to setting point, testing some on a saucer, and pour into clean hot jars, and seal.

FIVE FRUIT JELLY

You can almost use any fruit of your choice in this recipe, which is ideal if you have any fruit left in your freezer and you want to use it up.

225g (8 oz) each strawberries, raspberries, redcurrants, gooseberries and cherries
425ml (15fl oz) water   Sugar

Wash and clean over fruit. Put into a preserving pan, cover with water and simmer gently until fruit is soft – 25 – 30 minutes. Turn into a jelly bag or cloth and leave to drip until thoroughly drained. Measure the juice, making up to an even pint. Bring to the boil, take off heat and add 450g (1lb) sugar to each 600ml (1 pint) of juice. Bring to a rapid boil and boil until setting point is reached, about 10-15 minutes. Add half a lemon if you find the jelly is not setting quick enough. Pour into warmed jars and seal.

DAMSON JELLY

The damson is one of my favourite fruits, but I find that they are sometimes scarce to track down in supermarkets and shops. However, if you are lucky enough to have a damson tree or know a friend that has one, do try and make this jelly from this versatile little fruit.

2kg (4lb) damsons   Preserving sugar (I usually use granulated)
Juice of 2 lemons

Clean over fruit and put into a preserving pan with the lemon juice and 300ml (10fl oz) water. Bring slowly to the boil and simmer for about 35-40 minutes until the fruit is soft. Pour the liquid from the pan into a jelly bag with a large bowl underneath to catch the juice. Leave until all the juice has been drained into the pan. Measure the juice back into the pan and add 450g (1lb) sugar to every 600ml (1 pint) of juice. Stir over a very low heat until the sugar has dissolved, then raise the heat and boil rapidly until setting point is reached. Test by spooning a little on a cold saucer and, if it wrinkles when pushed with your finger, it is ready. Pot into warm jars and seal.

FRESH APRICOT JAM

When apricots are in season its nice to make some real apricot jam. I find the markets usually have plenty to sell around May to August when they start to come in from abroad and then at the end of the year December to February. Try to buy firm, and not bruised fruit, as it does make all the difference to the quality of your jam.

2kg (4½ lb) apricots   425ml (15fl oz) water
2kg (4½ lb) sugar

Wash fruit and remove stones. Put fruit into a preserving pan with the water. Remove the kernels from some of the stones and blanch them, add to the pan and simmer until the fruit is tender. Add the sugar and stir until dissolved. Then boil rapidly for about 15 minutes until setting point is reached. Pot into warm sterilised jars and seal.

RASPBERRY AND RHUBARB JAM

Raspberries and rhubarb go well together and I prefer this to the traditional rhubarb jam with crystallised ginger added.

1.4kg (3 lb) raspberries   600ml (1 pint) water
1.4kg (3 lb) rhubarb   2.7kg (6 lb) sugar

Clean over rhubarb and cut into small pieces and simmer in the water until soft. Add the raspberries and gently simmer until soft. Stir in the sugar until dissolved, then boil rapidly until it has reached setting point. Pour into hot jars, cover and seal.

MARROW JAM

If you find you have a glut of marrows then try using some of them to make this marrow jam. The name rather belies the flavour!

2kg (4½ lb) marrow   2 lemons, juice and rind
1.4kg (3 lb) preserving sugar   1 oz ground ginger

Peel marrow and cut into cubes. Place in a bowl, cover with the sugar and allow to stand overnight. Place in a preserving pan with lemon juice, grated rind and ground ginger. Simmer gently and stir well until it sets when tested on a cold saucer. (I find this jam rarely needs a rapid boil). Pour into hot jars and seal.

STRAWBERRY JAM

Lots of my friends find strawberry jam is hard to set, and I find I have to add extra lemon juice if setting point is taking too long. This old recipe seemed to do the trick and I found that by leaving the jam to get nearly cold helped the strawberries to settle more evenly in the jars.

1.8kg (4 lb) strawberries   Juice of 4 lemons
1.6kg (3½ lb) preserving sugar

Prepare the fruit by removing the stalks and hulls. Put into a preserving pan and add the juice of the lemons. Simmer until the fruit is thoroughly softened. Add the sugar and stir while boiling, about 15-20 minutes. Test on saucer in the usual way. Allow to get nearly cold, stirring frequently. Put into jars and seal.

PLUM JAM

Plums usually start to arrive in the shops around August and September and I find that the golden ones are the best for this jam.

2kg (4½ lb) golden plums   2kg (4½ lb) sugar
300ml (10fl oz) water

Wash fruit, then halve and stone the plums, reserving about 18 stones. Put the fruit into a preserving pan, and take out the kernels from the plum stones with a nut cracker and add them to the plums in the preserving pan, and then add the water. Gently heat over a low heat and slowly bring the liquid to the boil. Then lower the heat and simmer for about 40 – 45 minutes until the fruit has turned into a thick pulp. Add the sugar and stir until it is all dissolved. Bring the jam to the boil and continue to boil fairly rapidly until setting point has been reached. Then pour into hot jars, cover and seal.

SEVILLE MARMALADE

A quick and simple marmalade to make when the Sevilles come into our shops. I find buying double the quantity of Seville oranges and freezing them enables you to top up your marmalade store by making some in the warmer months when the Sevilles aren't around.

1.4k (3lb) Seville oranges   Juice of 2 lemons
2.25 litres (4 pints) water   2.7kg (6lb) sugar

Wash the fruit and put it whole and unpeeled into a preserving pan. Cover with water and bring to the boil, then simmer with the lid on the pan until the fruit is tender, about $1\frac{1}{2}$ - 2 hours. When the fruit has cooled cut it in half and remove the pips and cut up the fruit, retaining all the juice. Return the pips to the water and boil for a further 6 minutes. Put the sliced oranges with the liquid (strained free from pips) and adding the lemon juice into the preserving pan. Reduce the heat and add the sugar, which has been warmed and stir until dissolved.   Bring to a quick boil and boil rapidly until setting point is reached.

LEMON MARMALADE

A golden tangy flavoured marmalade, which is easy to make.

675g ($1\frac{1}{2}$ lb) lemons   1.4kg (3 lb) sugar

l.7 litres (3 pints) water

Wash the lemons thoroughly and shred the peel very finely, removing some of the pith if it is very thick. Cut up the fruit, putting aside the pips. Put the fruit and shredded peel into a large bowl with 1.5 litres ($2\frac{1}{2}$ pints) water. Put the pips and any coarse tissue in a separate basin covered with 300ml ($\frac{1}{2}$ pint) water. Leave all to soak for at least 24 hours.   Then transfer all to a preserving pan, tying the pips etc., in a muslin bag. Bring to the boil and simmer gently for about $1\frac{1}{2}$ hours until the peel is tender and the contents of the pan are reduced by at least one third. Remove the muslin bag and add the sugar, stir until dissolved and then bring to the boil and boil rapidly until setting point has been reached, about 15 – 20 minutes. Then pot in warm jars and seal.

ROSE PETAL AND RHUBARB JAM

This is one of the most delicious flavoured and red jewelled coloured jams I have ever made. Admittedly I don't make it often, but I just had to include in my new book.

110g (4 oz) dark red rose petals   Juice of 1 lemon

450g (1lb) rhubarb   450g (1lb) sugar

Clean over and cut up the rhubarb into small pieces and leave to stand overnight with the lemon juice and sugar. Cut the rose petals into pieces and add to the mixture. Bring to the boil and then boil to setting point. Pour into small hot jars, cover and seal. This jam is delicious on scones, or just plain bread and butter – real luxury!

APPLE CHUTNEY

Some years ago I found this recipe in a very old Devonshire W.I. book and I've been making it ever since!

1.4kg (3 lb) sour apples	2 lemons
700g (1½ lb) brown sugar	1 tablespoon mustard seed
450g (1lb) seedless raisins	Pepper and salt
900g (2 lb) onions	1½ litres (2 pints) malt vinegar
1 dessertspoon ginger	

Peel the apples and onions, and mince them with the raisins. Put this mixture into a preserving pan, and add the grated rind and strained juice of the lemons and all the other ingredients. Bring to the boil and simmer gently until tender, stirring frequently. Allow to cool before potting and sealing, and keep for 6 weeks before using.

BANANA CHUTNEY

In the village where my husband and I look after the Church Gift Shop we get asked for this chutney time and time again, but unfortunately our suppliers do not stock or make it. However, I was lucky to beg this recipe from a friend - it doesn't take much preparing or cooking, and is very good with all meats.

450g (1lb) mild onions	1 teaspoon curry powder
225g (8 oz) stoned dates	225g (8 oz) seedless raisins
6 bananas	600ml (1 pint) syrup from any tinned fruit
110g (4 oz) crystallised ginger	425ml (15fl oz) vinegar
1 teaspoon salt	

Mince onions, dates and bananas, and put into preserving pan with vinegar and simmer for 20 minutes. Add crystallised ginger, salt, curry powder, raisins and syrup. Cook until mixture thickens. Then cool and pot in warm jars and seal.

BLACKBERRY CHUTNEY

Until I was given this recipe by a friend I had never associated blackberries with chutney, but I find it does make an excellent accompaniment to cold meats and fish.

1.4kg (3lb) blackberries

700g (1½ lb) cooking apples

350g (12 oz) onions

600ml (1 pint) white vinegar

2 teaspoons ground ginger

1 teaspoon ground mace

1 teaspoon dry mustard

450g (1 lb) sugar

1 tablespoon salt

Pick and clean over the blackberries, wash well and drain. Peel, core and chop the apples and onions. Then place the blackberries, apples and onions in a pan with the vinegar and spices. Bring to the boil, then simmer gently until tender, stirring occasionally. If you want the chutney to be seedless, sieve at this stage and return the sieved mixture to a clean pan. Add the sugar and salt, and stir until dissolved. Return to the boil and cook gently until thick, stirring occasionally. Pot into warm jars and seal.

GREEN TOMATO CHUTNEY

It's always nice to have some pots of this popular chutney in your store cupboard, it keeps well too and goes with most cold meats.

900g (4 lb) green tomatoes

700g (1½ lb) shallots

450g (1lb) cooking apples

600ml (1 pint) vinegar

250g (8 oz) seedless raisins

12 red chillies

25g (1 oz) dried root ginger

2 teaspoons salt

450g (1 lb) sugar

Wash and finely chop the tomatoes. Peel and chop the shallots. Peel, core and chop the apples. Put the tomatoes, shallots and apples in a pan and add half the vinegar. Bruise the chillies and ginger and tie in a muslin bag. Add the raisins and spice bag to the pan and cook until soft and pulpy. Add the remaining vinegar, the salt and sugar and stir well. Continue cooking until thick, pressing the bag of spices occasionally with the wooden spoon. Remove the bag, pot into warm jars and cover.

TOMATO RELISH

This relish needs to be kept at least 6 weeks before using – it will taste all the better!

2kg (4 lb) ripe tomatoes	1 tablespoon mustard seeds
700g (1½ lb) onions	425ml (¾ pint) white wine vinegar
1 red pepper	450g (1 lb) granulated sugar
3 large celery stalks	25g (1 oz) salt

Peel and finely chop the tomatoes and onions. Mix together in a bowl and sprinkle with the salt, leave overnight. Next morning rinse the tomatoes and onions under cold running water and drain well. Clean and finely chop the celery. De-seed and finely chop the pepper, if used. Mix the celery and pepper together in a large bowl with the sugar, mustard seeds and vinegar. Stir in the tomatoes and onions. Pot into dry jars and cover. Keep at least six weeks before using.

CUCUMBER RELISH

This is a good way of using up those misshapen cucumbers which you can often find being sold cheaply in the markets and shops.

3 large cucumbers	175g (6 oz) sugar
4 medium onions	1 teaspoon celery seeds
50g (2 oz) cooking salt	1 teaspoon mustard seeds
600ml (1 pint) white vinegar	

Wipe the cucumbers, but do not peel them. Cut into small cubes. Peel and chop the onions. Layer the cucumber and onions in a bowl with the salt and leave for 1-2 hours. Tip into a colander and drain well. Put the vinegar, sugar and spices in a pan and stir to dissolve the sugar. Bring to the boil and simmer gently for 3-4 minutes. Pack the drained vegetables into warm jars and cover immediately with the hot vinegar mixture, including the spices. This relish can be used after about 4 weeks.

BEETROOT RELISH

This relish is a good one to put on a buffet table where cold meats are being served with salad.

450g (1lb) raw white cabbage

450g (1 lb) cooked, peeled beetroot

225 (8 oz) granulated sugar

2 tablespoons grated or dried horseradish

1 tablespoon dry mustard

Pinch of black pepper

1 teaspoon salt

600ml (1 pint) vinegar

Chop the beetroot roughly. Core and shred the cabbage. Put these in a pan with all the other ingredients and stir to dissolve the sugar. Simmer gently for 30 minutes. Pot into warm jars and cover. Keep for at least 6 weeks before using.

IMPERIAL/METRIC EQUIVALENTS

VOLUME
11/4ml .... $\frac{1}{4}$tsp
21/2ml .... $\frac{1}{2}$tsp
5ml .... 1 level tsp
15ml ...... 1 level tbsp
30ml .... 1 fl oz
50ml .... 2 fl oz
150ml .... 5 fl oz .... $\frac{1}{4}$ pint
200ml .... 7 fl oz .... $\frac{1}{3}$ pint
300ml .... 10 fl oz .... $\frac{1}{2}$ pint
425ml .... 15 fl oz .... $\frac{3}{4}$ pint
600ml .... 20 fl oz .... 1 pint
700ml ....$1\frac{1}{4}$ pints
850ml ....$1\frac{1}{2}$ pints
1 litre ....$1\frac{3}{4}$ pints
11/2litres .... 2 pints
2 litres .... $3\frac{1}{2}$ pints

WEIGHT
10g .... $\frac{1}{2}$oz
20g .... $\frac{3}{4}$oz
25g 1oz
50g 2oz
75g 3oz
110g 4oz
150g 5oz
175g 6oz
200g 7oz
225g 8oz
250g 9oz
275g .... $9\frac{1}{2}$oz
300g .... $10\frac{1}{2}$oz
350g 12oz
375g 13oz
400g 14oz
425g 15oz
450g 1lb
700g .... $1\frac{1}{2}$lb
750g 1lb 10oz
1kg .... $2\frac{1}{4}$lb
11/4kg 2lb 12oz
11/2kg 3lb 5oz
2kg .... $4\frac{1}{2}$lb
21/4kg 5lb
21/2kg 5lb 8oz
3kg 6lb 8oz

MEASUREMENT
3mm .... $\frac{1}{8}$in
5mm .... $\frac{1}{4}$in
1cm .... $\frac{1}{2}$in
2cm .... $\frac{3}{4}$in
2.5cm 1in
3cm .... $1\frac{1}{4}$in
4cm .... $1\frac{1}{2}$in
5cm 2in
6cm .... $2\frac{1}{2}$in
7.5cm .... $2\frac{3}{4}$in
9cm .... $3\frac{1}{2}$in
10cm 4in
11.5cm .... $4\frac{1}{2}$in
12.5cm 5in
15cm 6in
17cm .... $6\frac{1}{2}$in
18cm 7in
20.5cm 8in
23cm 9in
24cm .... $9\frac{1}{2}$in
25.5 .... 10in
30.5cm 12in

AMERICAN CUP MEASURES
Butter, margarine, lard
25g .... 2 tbsp ...... $\frac{1}{4}$ stick
100g .... 8 tbsp .... 1 stick

Breadcrumbs
Fresh 50g .... 1 cup
Dried 115g .... 1 cup

Cheese
Grated cheddar 115g .... 1 cup
Dice cheddar 170g .... 1 cup
Parmesan 150g .... 1 cup
Cream cheese 225g .... 1 cup

Dried Fruit
Currants, sultanas 150g .... 1 cup
Apricots 150-175g .... 1 cup
Prunes 175g .... 1 cup
Glace cherries 125g .... 1 cup

Fish
Prawns, peeled 175g .... 1 cup
Cooked and flaked 225g .... 1 cup

Flour
Cornflour 25g .... $\frac{1}{4}$ cup
Firmly packed flour 115g ...... 1 cup

Liquids
Syrup, treacle, honey 350g .... 1 cup
Liquids 225ml .... 1 cup

Meat
Meat, minced & packed 225g 1 cup

Nuts
Almonds, whole/shelled 150g 1 cup
Almonds, flaked 115g .... 1 cup
Grounds nuts 115g .... 1 cup
Hazelnuts 150g .... 1 cup
Walnuts and pecans 115g ...... 1 cup
Chopped nuts 115g .... 1 cup

Oats
Rolled oats 100g .... 1 cup
Oatmeal 175g .... 1 cup

Pulses
Split peas, lentils 225g .... 1 cup
Haricot beans 200g .... 1 cup
Kidney beans 300g .... 1 cup

Rice
Uncooked 200g .... 1 cup
Cooked and drained 165g .... 1 cup
Semolina, ground rice and
couscous 175g .... 1 cup

Sugar
Caster & granulated 225g ...... 1 cup
Moist brown 200g .... 1 cup
Icing sugar 125g .... 1 cup

Vegetables
Onions, chopped 115g .... 1 cup
Cabbage, shredded 75g .... 1 cup
Peas, shelled 150g .... 1 cup
Beansprouts 50g .... 1 cup
Potatoes, peeled & diced 170g 1 cup
Potatoes, mashed 225g .... 1 cup
Spinach, cooked puree 200-225g 1 cup
Tomatoes 225g .... 1 cup

MAXIMUM REFRIGERATOR STORAGE TIMES

The correct working temperature for a fridge is less than 5°C.

Raw meats

Joints .... 3 days
Poultry .... 2 days
Raw sliced meat .... 2 days
Minced meat .... 1 day
Offal .... 1 day
Sausages .... 3 days
Bacon .... 7 days
Raw fish .... 1 day

Cooked meats

Joints .... 3 days
Casseroles .... 2 days
Sliced meat .... 2 days
Ham .... 2 days
Cooked fish .... 1 day

Dairy foods

Milk .... 4-5 days
Cheese, soft .... 2-3 days
Cheese, hard .... 7-14 days
Eggs, raw .... 2 wks
Eggs, hard boiled .... 2 days
Freshly squeezed fruit juice ...... 1 day
Cooked vegetables .... 2 days
Cooked potatoes .... 2 days
Canned foods .... 2 days*

THAWING TIMES

At room temperature.

Meat

Joints over 1.5kg (3.3lb) .... 2-3 hrs
Cooked and flaked 225g .... 1-2 hrs

Poultry

All birds (min 9hrs) per 450g 31/2 hrs

Vegetables

Cook from frozen

FREEZER STORAGE

Meat and poultry

Sausage & sausage meat 2-3mths
Minced beef 3-4mths
Offal 3-4mths
Ham and bacon joints 3-4mths
Beef, lamb, pork and veal 4-6mths
Duck, goose & rabbit 4-6mths
Chicken, turkey & venison 10-12mths

Fish

Shellfish 2-3mths
Oily fish 3-4mths
White fish 6-8mths

Fruit & Vegetables

Fruit juice 4-6mths
Mushrooms & tomatoes 6-8mths
Vegetables purees 6-8mths
Fruit 8-10mths
Most vegetables 10-12mths

Dairy produce

Cream 6-8mths
Butter, unsalted 6-8mths
Butter, salted 3-4mths
Cheese, hard 4-6mths
Cheese, soft 3-4mths
Ice cream 3-4mths
Milk, skimmed 3-4mths
Milk, semi-skimmed 3-4mths

Ready-prepared meals

Ready-prepared meals 4-6mths
Highly seasoned 2-3mths
Cakes 4-6mths
Bread 2-3mths
Bread dough 2-3mths

Guidelines for refridgerator and freezer storage and thawing times were provided by the Food Safety Advisory Centre. Volume and weight values are inline with the British Weights & Measures Association.

*Once opened, canned foods should be trans-ferred to a clean, dry container with a lid.

Oven Temperatures

Celsius	Fahrenheit	Gas	Description
110°C	225°C	mark 1/4	cool
130°C	250°C	mark 1/2	cool
140°C	275°C	mark 1	very low
150°C	300°C	mark 2	very low
170°C	325°C	mark 3	low
180°C	350°C	mark 4	moderate
190°C	375°C	mark 5	moderately
200°C	400°C	mark 6	hot
220°C	425°C	mark 7	hot
230°C	450°C	mark 8	very hot

For fan-assisted ovens reduce temperatures 10°C

Roasting Times for Meat And Poultry

Use these times as a guide but always check that pork and poultry are cooked through.

Beef		
Rare	20 mins per 450g (1lb) plus 20 mins	180°C (350°F)
Medium	25 mins per 450g (1lb) plus 25 mins	180°C (350°F)
Well done	30 mins per 450g (1lb) plus 30 mins	180°C (350°F)
Pork		
Medium	30 mins per 450g (1lb) plus 30 mins	180°C (350°F)
Well done	35 mins per 450g (1lb) plus 35 mins	180°C (350°F)
Lamb		
Medium	25 mins per 450g (1lb) plus 25 mins	180°C (350°F)
Well done	30 mins per 450g (1lb) plus 30 mins	180°C (350°F)
Poultry		
Well done	18 mins per 450g (1lb) plus 30 mins	190°C (375°F)

*Smaller joints weighing less than 1.25kg (2lb 12oz) may require 5 mins per 450g (1lb) extra cooking time.

USEFUL CONVERSION CHART

i.e. cooking by an Aga,electricity or gas

If you cook by an Aga or, like me, you cook by an electric cooker as well, these are the guidelines you should use when converting from cooking by electricity to cooking by an Aga.

Roasting Oven (Top Half)	400F-425F	200C-220C	**Gas Mark 6-7**
Roasting Oven (Lower Half)	350F-375F	180C-190C	**Gas Mark 4-5**
Baking Oven (Top Half)	325F-350F	170C-180C	**Gas Mark Low-Moderate**
Baking Oven (Lower Half)	225F-250F	110C-130C	**Gas Mark 1/4-1/2**
Simmering Oven	225F-110C	**Gas 1/4 Cool**	

I find if I am roasting a joint or chicken, weight 2kg (41/2lb), in my Two-Oven Aga, it's best to put the meat, smeared with a little oil or butter and covered with foil, in the roasting oven, bottom half, for approximately 1 hour 40 minutes, and finish cooking with foil removed for the last 15 minutes of cooking time. To make sure the meat is cooked, test with a skewer and if the juices run clear, then it's cooked, but if they run pink then it isn't. You can always leave your joint or chicken in the oven a bit longer if you want to crisp the meat up more.

Remember to use your cold shelf as directed in your Aga Book. This shelf should be kept outside your Aga, but I must admit I always seem to keep mine in the simmering oven, and so far I haven't noticed any problems with my baking when I've used it in the roasting oven. Good luck with your cooking what ever method you use!

SEASONS –

Fruits and Vegetables

WHEN FRUITS ARE IN SEASON

This is to show when British-grown fruit is available.

	Jan	Feb	Mar	Apr	May	June	July	Aug	Sept	Oct	Nov	Dec
Apples –												
Cooking	•	•	•	•	•	•			•	•	•	•
Dessert	•	•	•							•		•
Blackberries									•	•		
Black/redcurrants						•	•	•				
Crab apples									•	•		
Cherries						•	•	•				
Chestnuts										•	•	•
Damsons								•	•	•		
Elderberries									•	•		
Gooseberries						•	•	•				
Greengages							•	•				
Loganberries							•	•				
Medlars										•	•	
Mulberries							•	•				
Pears	•	•	•					•	•	•	•	•
Plums							•	•	•	•		
Quinces										•	•	
Raspberries						•	•	•	•			
Rhubarb		•	•	•	•							
Strawberries					•	•	•	•	•	•		

WHEN VEGETABLES ARE IN SEASON

This is to show when British-grown vegetables are available.

	Jan	Feb	Mar	Apr	May	June	July	Aug	Sept	Oct	Nov	Dec
Artichokes –												
Globe						•	•	•	•			
Jerusalem	•	•	•	•						•	•	•
Asparagus					•	•						
Beans –												
Broad						•	•					
Runner							•	•	•			
Kidney						•	•	•	•			
Beetroot	•	•	•	•	•	•	•	•	•	•	•	•
Broccoli –												
Calabrese						•	•	•	•			
Sprouting			•	•	•							
Brussels –												
Top	•									•	•	•
Sprouts	•	•	•	•						•	•	•
Cabbage –												
January King	•	•	•	•						•	•	•
Drum Head							•		•	•		
Spring Green	•	•	•							•	•	•
Red	•	•										•
Carrot	•	•	•	•	•	•	•	•	•	•	•	•
Cauliflower	•	•	•	•	•	•	•	•	•	•	•	•
Celeriac	•	•	•						•	•		•
Celery					•	•	•	•	•	•	•	•
Chicory	•	•							•	•	•	
Chinese Leaves					•	•	•	•	•	•	•	
Courgettes						•	•	•	•	•		
Cucumbers				•	•	•	•	•	•	•		
Endive					•	•	•	•				
Kale	•	•	•	•	•						•	•

	Jan	Feb	Mar	Apr	May	June	July	Aug	Sept	Oct	Nov	Dec
Leeks	•	•	•	•				•	•	•	•	•
Lettuce	•	•	•	•	•	•	•	•	•	•	•	•
Marrows						•	•	•	•	•		
Mint					•	•	•	•	•	•		
Mushrooms	•	•	•	•	•	•	•	•	•	•	•	•
Mustard and Cress	•	•	•	•	•	•	•	•	•	•	•	•
Onions	•								•	•	•	•
Parsley					•	•	•	•	•	•		
Parsnips	•	•	•	•					•	•	•	•
Peppers					•	•	•	•	•	•		
Peas					•	•	•	•	•	•		
Potatoes – New						•	•	•				
Maincrop	•	•	•	•	•				•	•	•	•
Pumpkin								•	•	•		
Radishes					•	•	•	•	•	•		
Seakale	•	•	•									•
Shallots	•								•	•	•	•
Spinach (best Mar/Apr)			•	•	•	•	•	•	•	•		
Spring onions					•	•	•	•	•			
Swedes	•	•	•	•	•				•	•	•	•
Sweetcorn								•	•	•		
Tomatoes					•	•	•	•	•	•		
Turnips	•	•	•			•	•	•	•	•	•	•
Watercress	•	•	•	•	•	•	•	•	•	•	•	•

FOR YOUR NOTES

FOR YOUR NOTES

FOR YOUR NOTES